MS Excel

Davinder Singh Minhas

RISING SUN
an imprint of
New Dawn Press

NEW DAWN PRESS GROUP
New Dawn Press, Inc., 244 South Randall Rd # 90, Elgin, IL 60123
e-mail: sales@newdawnpress.com
New Dawn Press, 2 Tintern Close, Slough, Berkshire, SL1-2TB, UK
e-mail: ndpuk@newdawnpress.com
sterlingdis@yahoo.co.uk

New Dawn Press (An Imprint of Sterling Publishers (P) Ltd.)

A-59, Okhla Industrial Area, Phase-II, New Delhi-110020
e-mail: sterlingpublishers@touchtelindia.net
Ghai@nde.vsnl.net.in

© 2005, New Dawn Press

All rights are reserved. No part of this publication may be reproduced, stored in a retrieval system or transmitted, in any form or by any means, mechanical, photocopying, recording or otherwise, without prior written permission of the publisher.

Printed at Sterling Publishers (P) Ltd., New Delhi-110020.

Contents

1. Introduction — 5
2. Working with Worksheet — 11
3. Save, Open and Edit the Worksheet — 18
4. Formula and Function — 25
5. Formatting the Worksheet — 34
6. Working with Charts — 37

1. Introduction

Microsoft Excel is a powerful spreadsheet program that allows you to organize and graph data, complete calculations, make decisions, develop reports, publish data on the Web, and access real-time data from Web sites. The four major parts of Excel are:

Worksheets

Worksheets or spreadsheets allow you to enter, calculate, manipulate and analyze data, such as numbers and text.

Charts

Charts are used to make a pictorial presentation of data. Excel can draw a variety of two-dimensional and three-dimensional charts.

Databases

Database are used to manage data. For example, once you enter data onto a worksheet, Excel can sort the data, search for specific data and select data that satisfies certain criteria.

Web Support

You can also access real-time data using Web queries. Web support allows Excel to save workbooks or parts of a workbook in HTML format so they can be viewed and manipulated using a browser.

Drag and Drop Series

Starting Excel

In order to start Excel, perform the following steps:

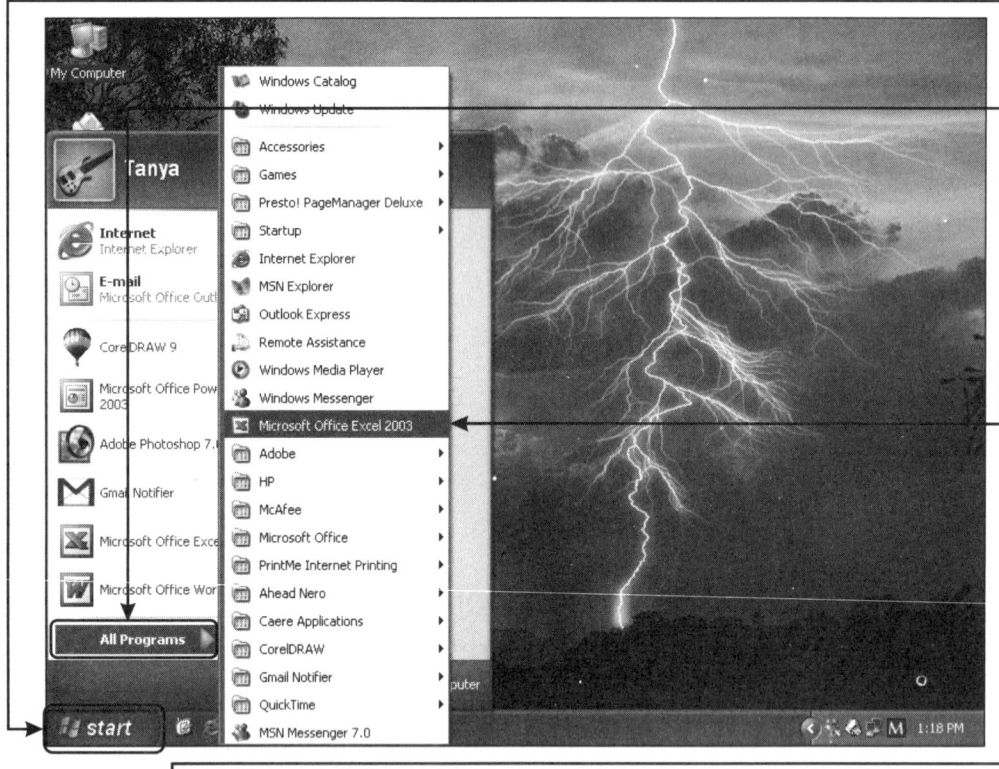

1. Click on the **Start** button. The Start menu will appear.

2. Click on **All Programs**.

3. In the All Programs submenu, click on **Microsoft Office Excel 2003**.

The Microsoft Excel window appears after a few moments.

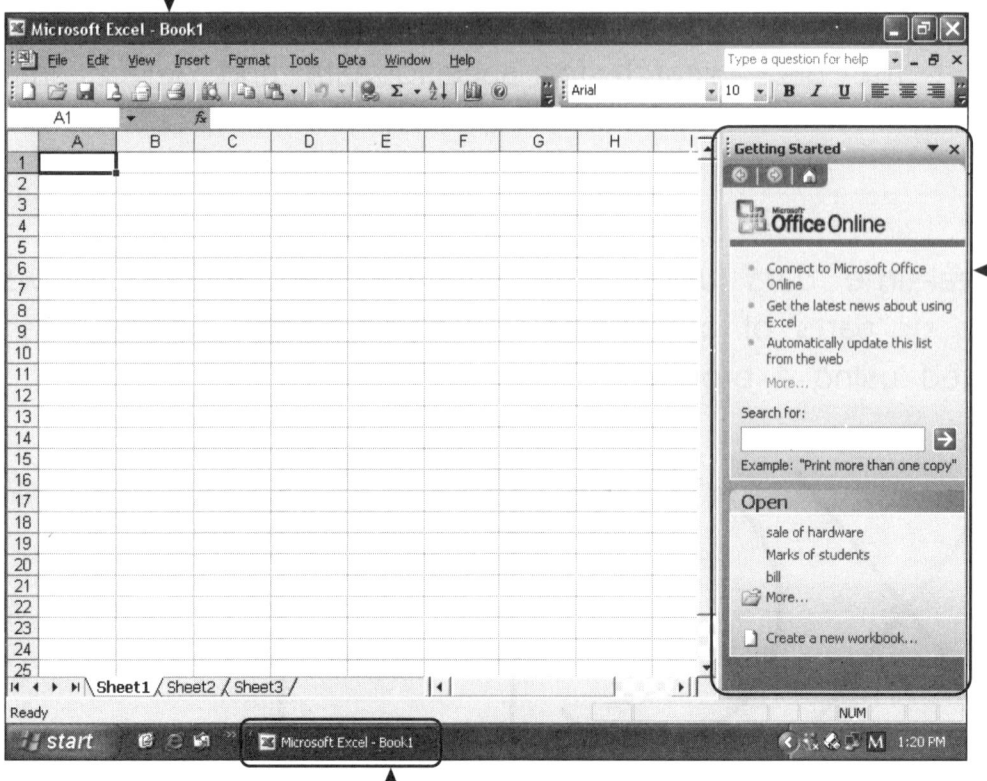

An empty Workbook titled **Book 1** is displayed in the Excel window.

A task pane may appear to perform common and online tasks very quickly.

The Window's taskbar displays the Excel program button, indicating that Excel is running.

6

The Excel Worksheet

A blank workbook is displayed when you open a new Excel document and is named **Book 1**. The **workbook** looks like a notebook and contains sheets, called **worksheets**. A new workbook contains three worksheets and up to 255 additional worksheets can also be added. Each sheet has a name displayed on a **sheet tab** at the bottom of the workbook.

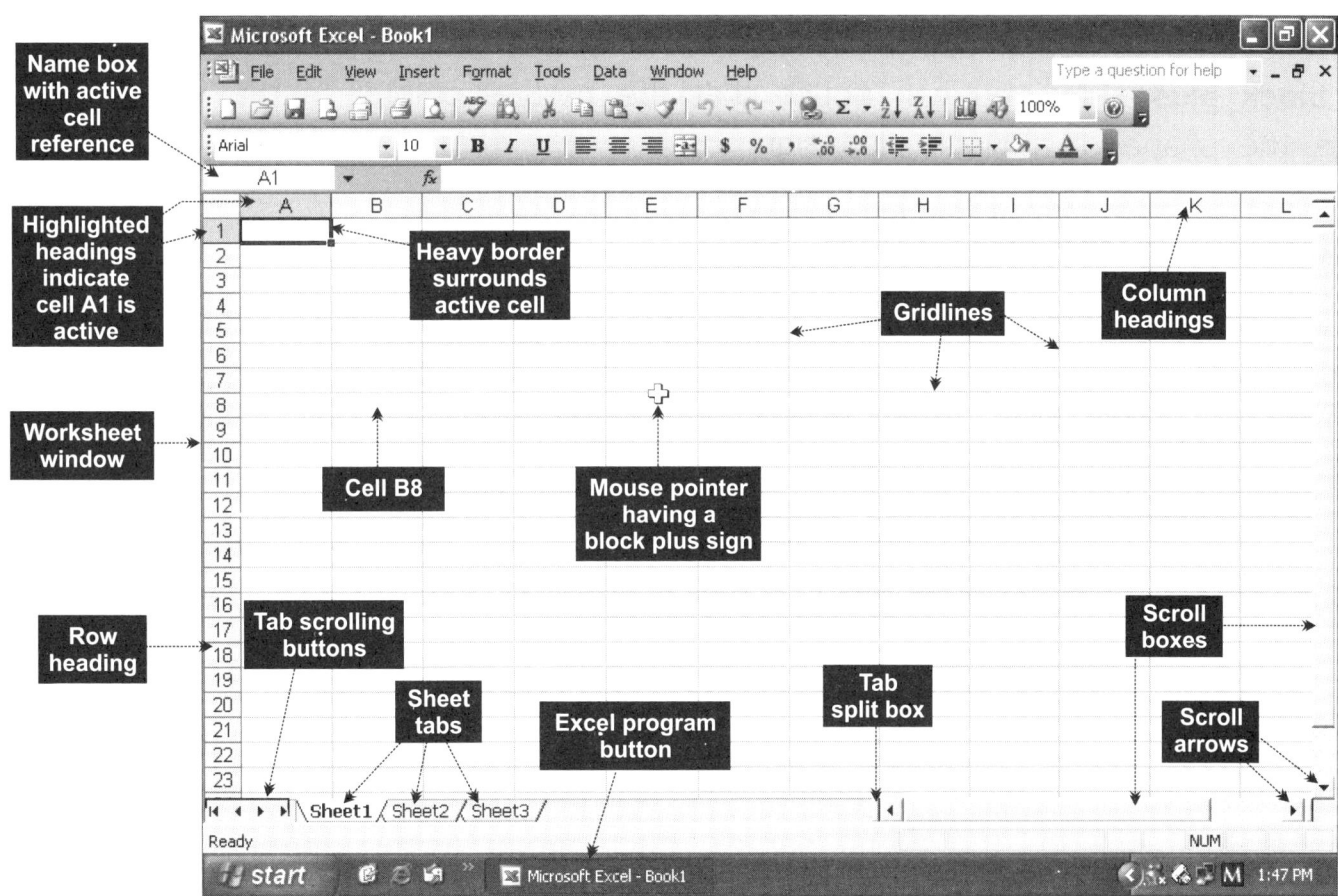

A worksheet is organized into a rectangular grid containing **columns** (vertical) and **rows** (horizontal). For identifying a column, there is a **column letter / column heading** above the grid. For identifying a row, there is a **row number / row heading** on the left side of the grid. The intersection of each column and row within a worksheet is called a **cell** and it is the basic unit into which you enter data. Each worksheet in a workbook has 256 columns and 65,536 rows, for a total of 16,777,216 cells. The column headings begin with 'A' and end with 'IV'. The row headings begin with 1 and end with 65,536. At one time only a small fraction of the active worksheet is displayed on the screen.

Drag and Drop Series

The coordinates of the intersecting column and row are known as **cell address** or **cell reference**. To identify a cell, specify the column letter first, followed by the row number. For example, cell reference B8 refers to the cell located at the intersection of column B and row 8.

For entering data, a cell in your worksheet is activated or selected by you. The active cell in the picture shown on the previous page is **A1**.

Whenever the mouse pointer is located in a cell on the worksheet, it displays a **block plus sign**. You can notice that the mouse pointer in the earlier picture has the shape of a block plus sign.

Worksheet Window

A worksheet window allows you to view the portion of the worksheet displayed on the screen. To move the window around to view different parts of the active worksheet, **scroll bars**, **scroll arrows** and **scroll boxes** located below and to the right of the worksheet are used.

At the top of the screen, just below the Title bar, the **Menu bar**, **Standard toolbar**, **Formatting toolbar**, **Formula bar** and **Ask a question box** are displayed.

Menu Bar

When you open an Excel worksheet you will find a **Menu bar,** which is a special toolbar that includes the menu names. Each **menu name** represents a menu of certain commands that you can use to open, store, print and format data on the worksheet. To display a menu, such as the Edit menu, click the Edit menu name on the menu bar. A **menu** is a list of commands. If you point to a command on the menu with an arrow to its right, a **submenu** is displayed from which you can choose a command.

When you click a menu bar, a **short menu** displays the list of the most recently used commands. If you wait for a few seconds or click the arrows at the bottom of the short menu, the full menu is displayed. The **full menu** lists all the commands associated with a menu.

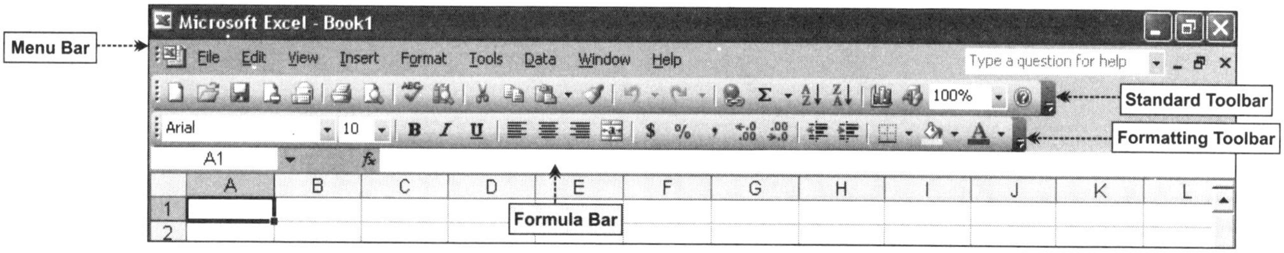

Excel

Menu Bar and Toolbar

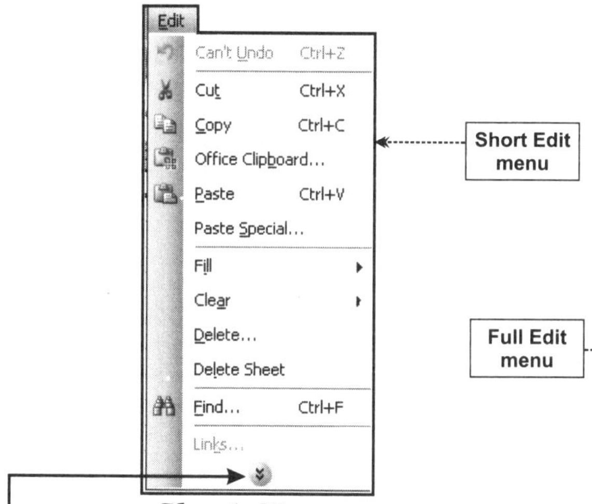

Short Menu

Click on the double down arrow to display Full Edit menu.

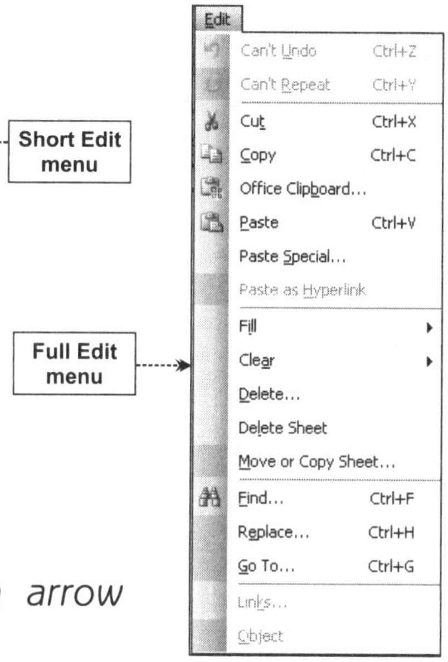

Full Menu

While working on an Excel sheet, a menu bar can be changed to include other menu names depending on the type of work. For example, if you are working with a chart sheet rather than a worksheet, the Chart menu bar is displayed with the menu names that shows the chart commands.

Standard and Formatting Toolbar

The **Standard toolbar** and the **Formatting toolbar** contain buttons and list boxes that allow you to perform tasks more quickly than using the menu bar.

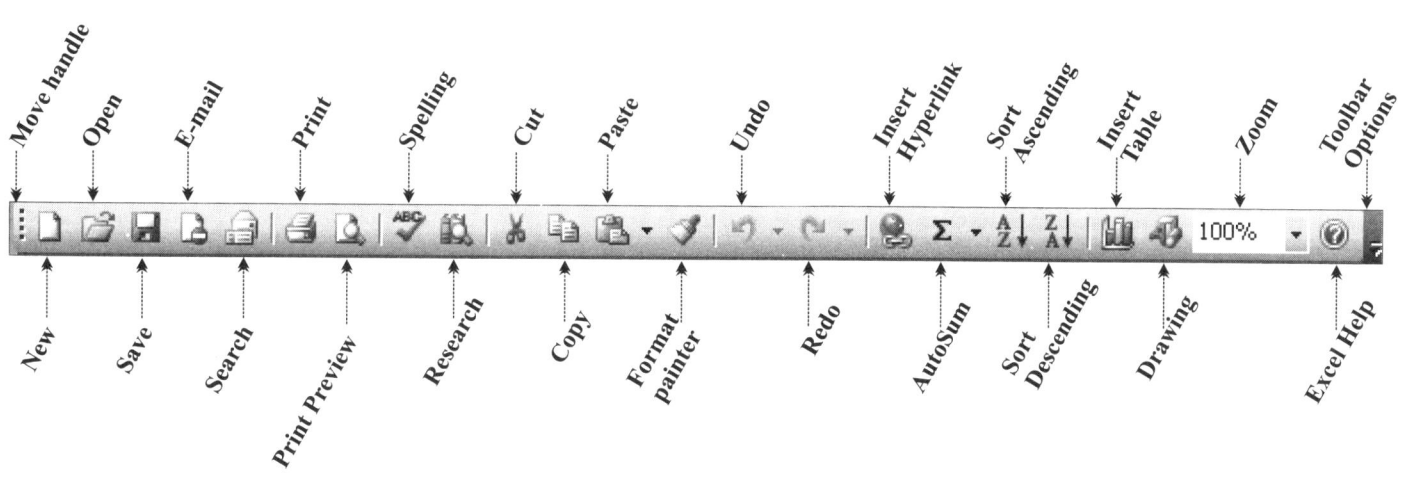

Standard Toolbar

9

Drag and Drop Series

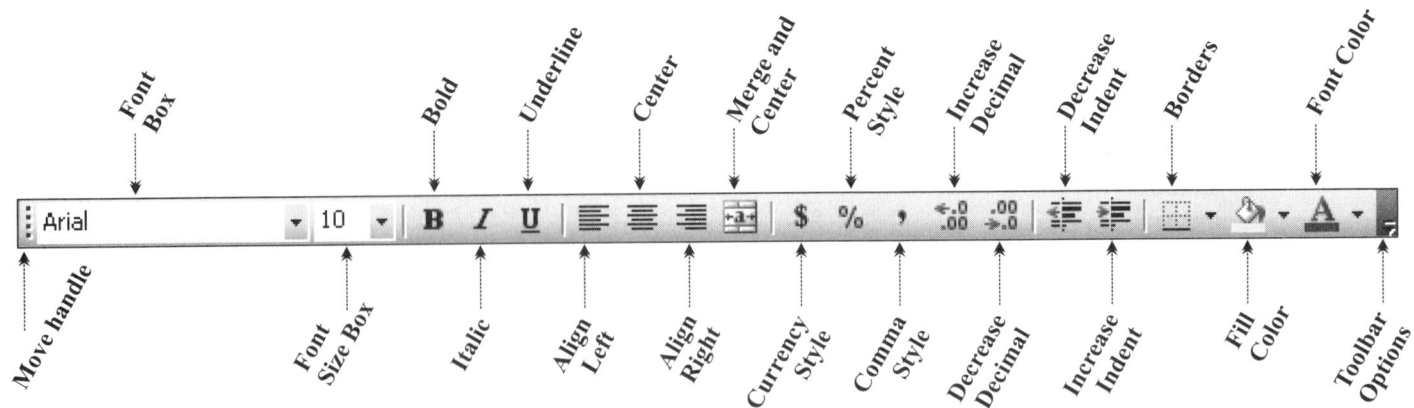

Formatting Toolbar

Formula Bar

Whatever data you type, it gets displayed in the **Formula bar**. The Formula bar appears below the Standard and Formatting toolbars. Excel also displays the active cell reference on the left side of the Formula bar in the Name box.

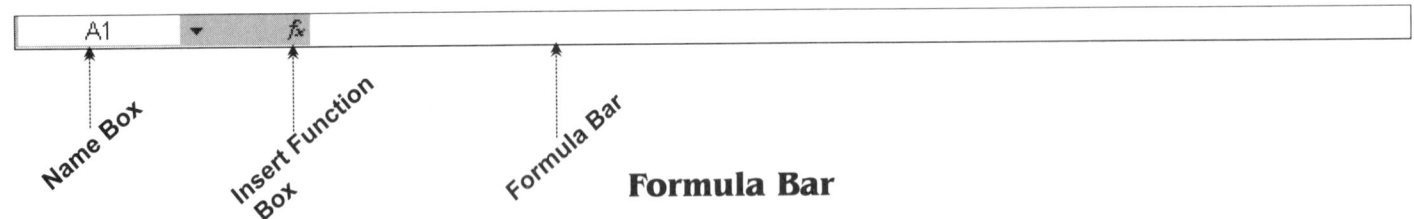

Formula Bar

Status Bar

The bar, which is positioned immediately above the Windows taskbar at the bottom of the screen is the **Status bar**. It displays the command selected (highlighted) in a menu, the execution of a function, and the mode of Excel.

AutoCalculate area is the middle space of the status bar. It can be used in place of a calculator to view the sum, average or the total of a group of numbers on the worksheet.

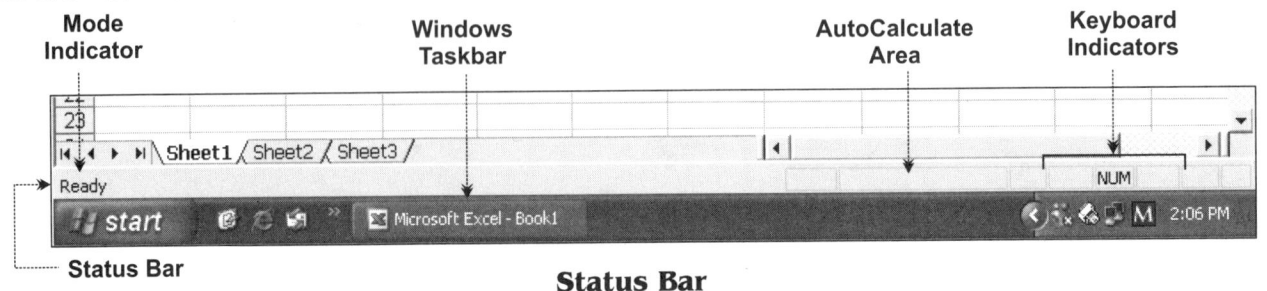

Status Bar

10

2. Working with Worksheet

Changing the Active Cell

You can make any cell in your worksheet the active cell and enter data into it.

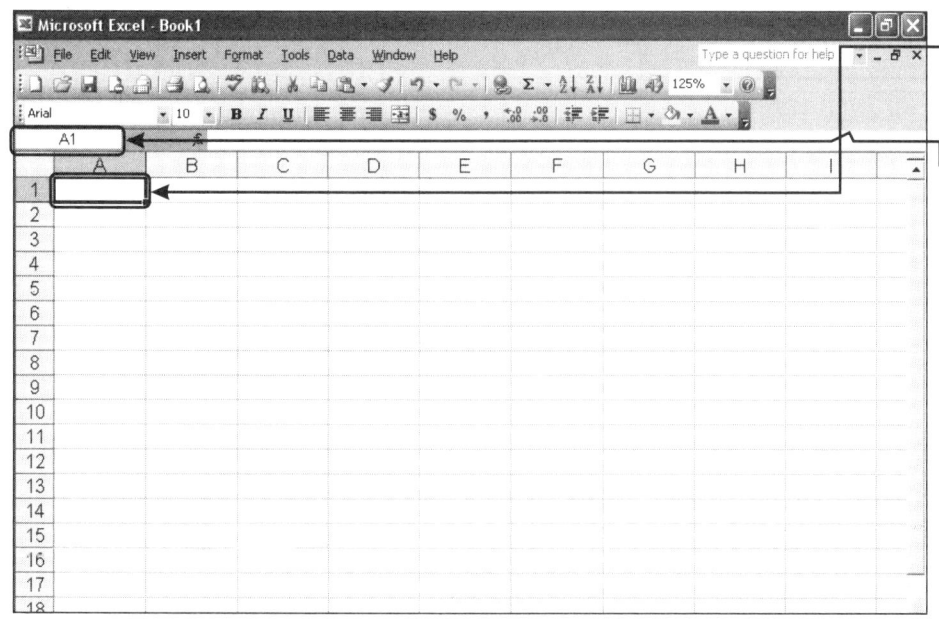

The active cell displays a thick border.

The cell reference for the active cell appears in this area. A cell reference identifies the location of each cell in a worksheet and consists of a column letter followed by a row number (example: A1).

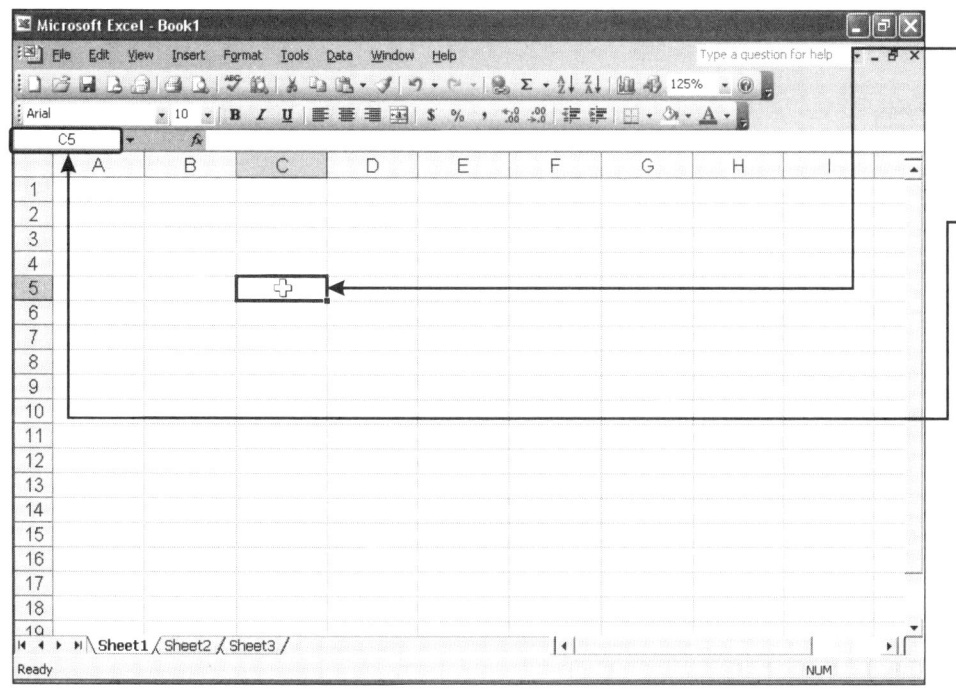

1. Click on the cell or use the arrow keys to mark the active cell.

The cell reference for the new active cell appears in this area.

Drag and Drop Series

Entering Data

Entering data is the first step in creating a worksheet. Depending on the requirement this data can be in the form of numbers or text. The simplest method is to click on a cell and begin typing. Once you press **Enter** or click on a different cell, the data is entered into the cell.

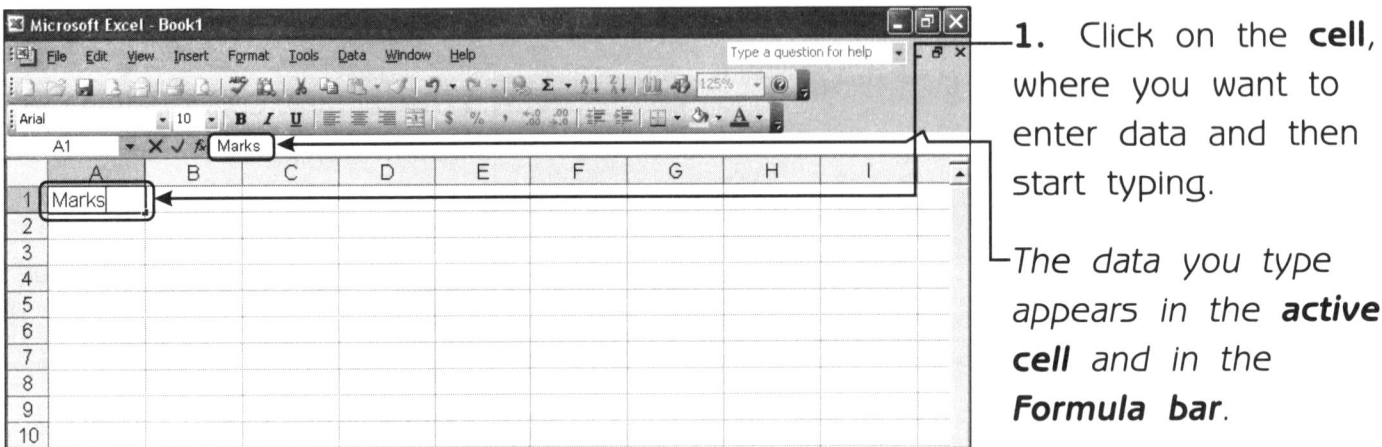

1. Click on the **cell**, where you want to enter data and then start typing.

The data you type appears in the **active cell** and in the **Formula bar**.

If you make a typing mistake while entering data, press the **Backspace** key from keyboard to remove the incorrect data. Then type the correct data.

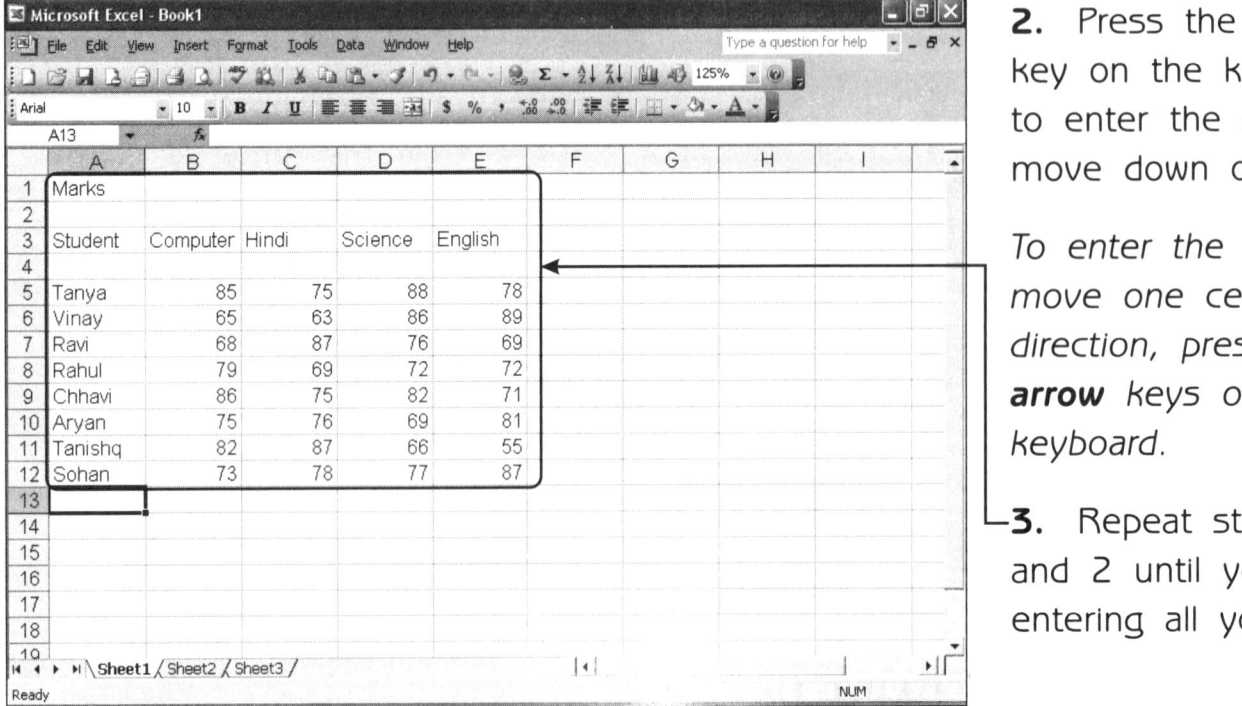

2. Press the **Enter** key on the keyboard to enter the data and move down one cell.

To enter the data and move one cell in any direction, press the **arrow** keys on the keyboard.

3. Repeat steps 1 and 2 until you finish entering all your data.

Excel

Selecting Cells

Before entering data, you must select a cell. The easiest way to select a cell or make it active is to use the mouse to move the block plus sign to the cell and then click on it.

An alternative method of selecting a cell in a worksheet is by using the **arrow keys** that are located on the keyboard. An arrow key selects the cell adjacent to the active cell in the direction of the arrow on the key.

You must select the cells you want to work with before performing any further tasks. Selected cells are highlighted on your screen.

To Select a Cell

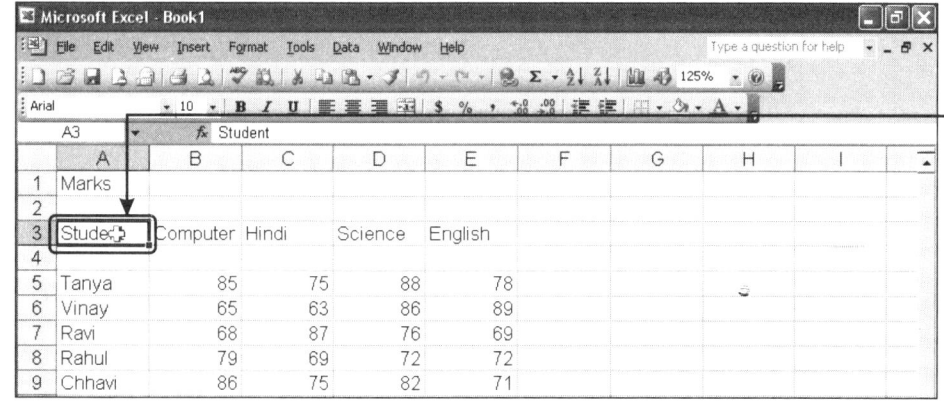

1. Click on the cell you want to select.

   The cell becomes the active cell and displays a thick border.

To Select a Row

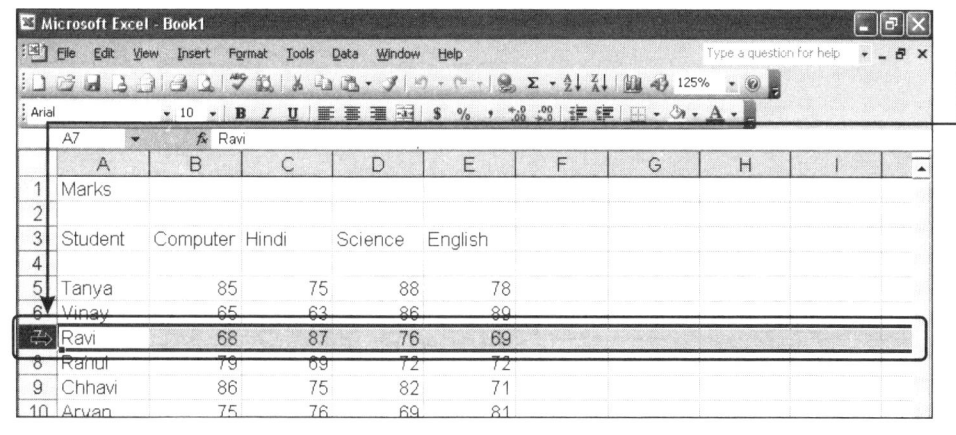

1. Click on the number of the row you want to select. The mouse pointer will change its shape (→).

   To select multiple rows, place your

mouse pointer (→) over the number of the first row you want to select. Then drag the mouse pointer (→) until you highlight all the rows you want to select.

13

Drag and Drop Series

To Select a Column

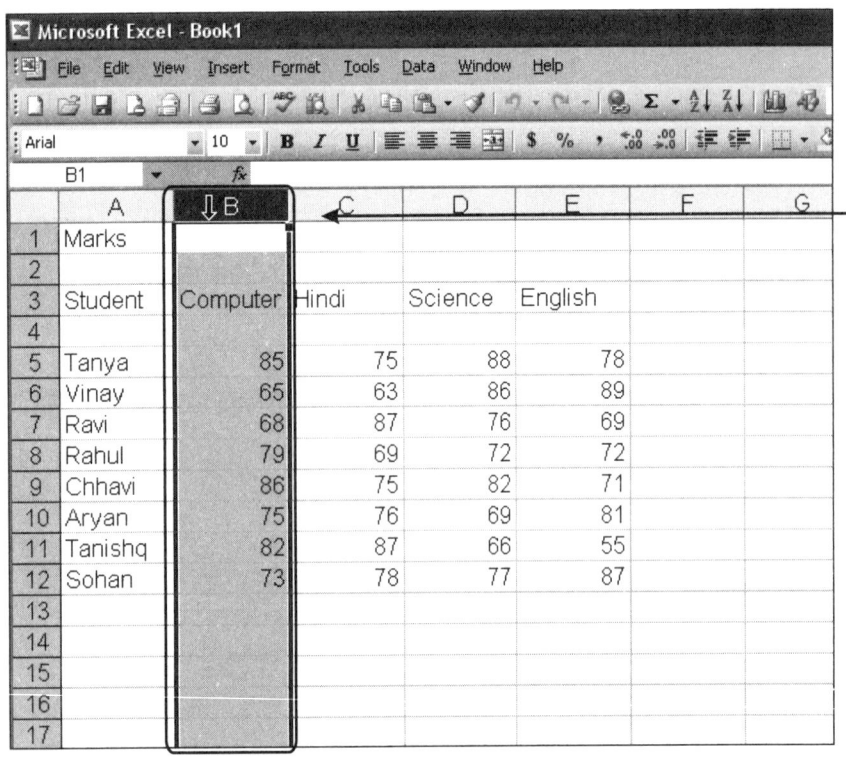

1. Click on the letter of the column you want to select.

To select multiple columns, position the mouse pointer (↓) over the letter of the first column you want to select. Then, drag the mouse pointer (↓) until you highlight all the columns you want to select.

To Select a Group of Cells

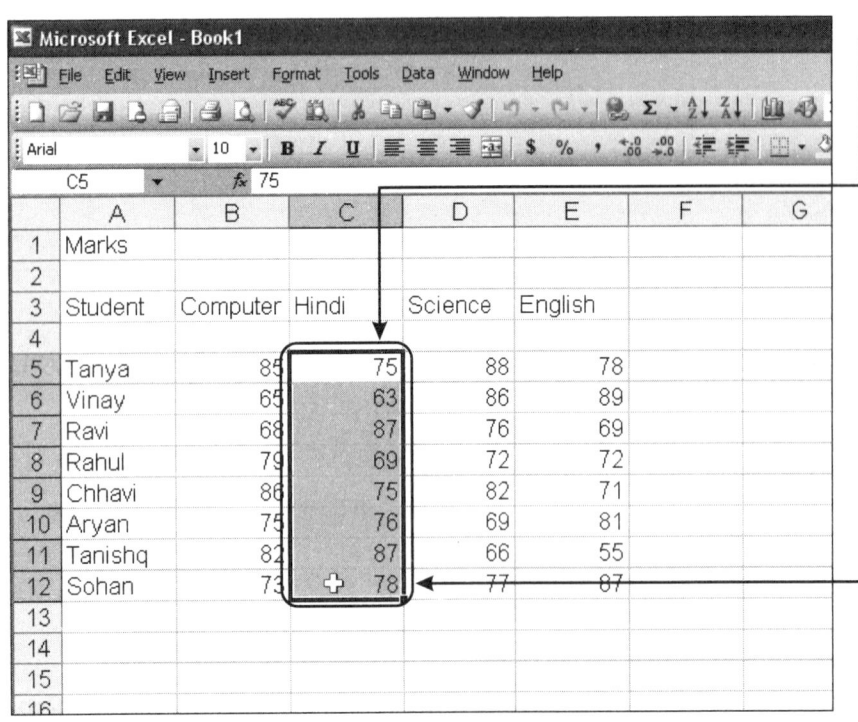

1. Place your mouse pointer (✢) over the first cell you want to select.

2. Drag the mouse pointer (✢) until you highlight all the cells you want to select.

*To select multiple groups of cells, press and hold down the **Ctrl** key as you repeat steps **1** and **2** for each group of cells you want to select.*

To deselect cells, click on any cell.

14

Excel

Completing a Series

By completing a text or number series, Excel can save your time. You can complete a series across a row or down a column in a worksheet. One of the most useful features is **Data Fill** which lets you fill in a range of cells based on some already entered data into an adjacent cell. For example, entries in a worksheet are based on daily inputs. You can use Data Fill to automate the process, rather than manually typing the date on every single row.

Text Series

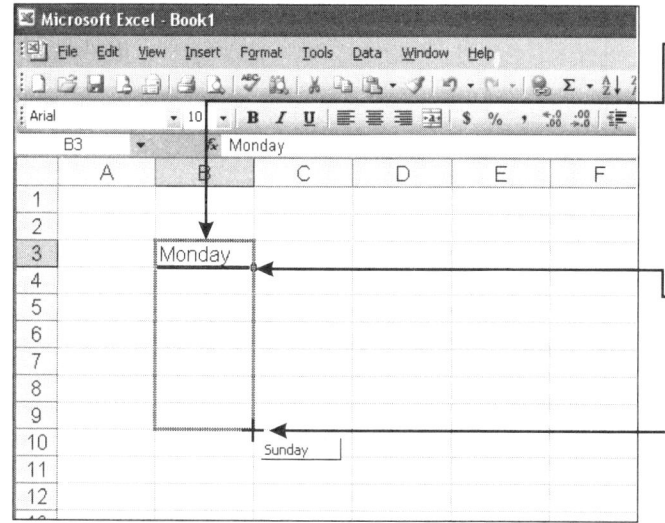

1. Enter the text you want to start the series with, eg Monday.

2. Click on the cell containing the text you entered.

3. Position the mouse over the bottom right corner of the cell.

4. Drag the mouse (+) over the cells you want to include in the series.

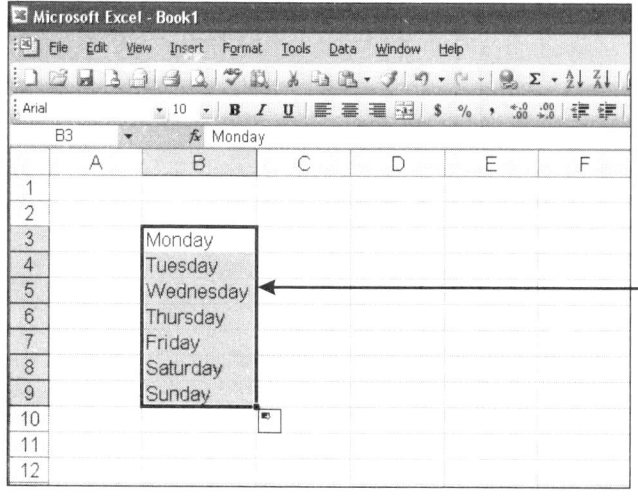

The cells display the text series.

If Excel cannot determine the text series you want to complete, it will copy the text in the first cell to all the cells you select.

To deselect the cells, click on any cell.

Drag and Drop Series

Number Series

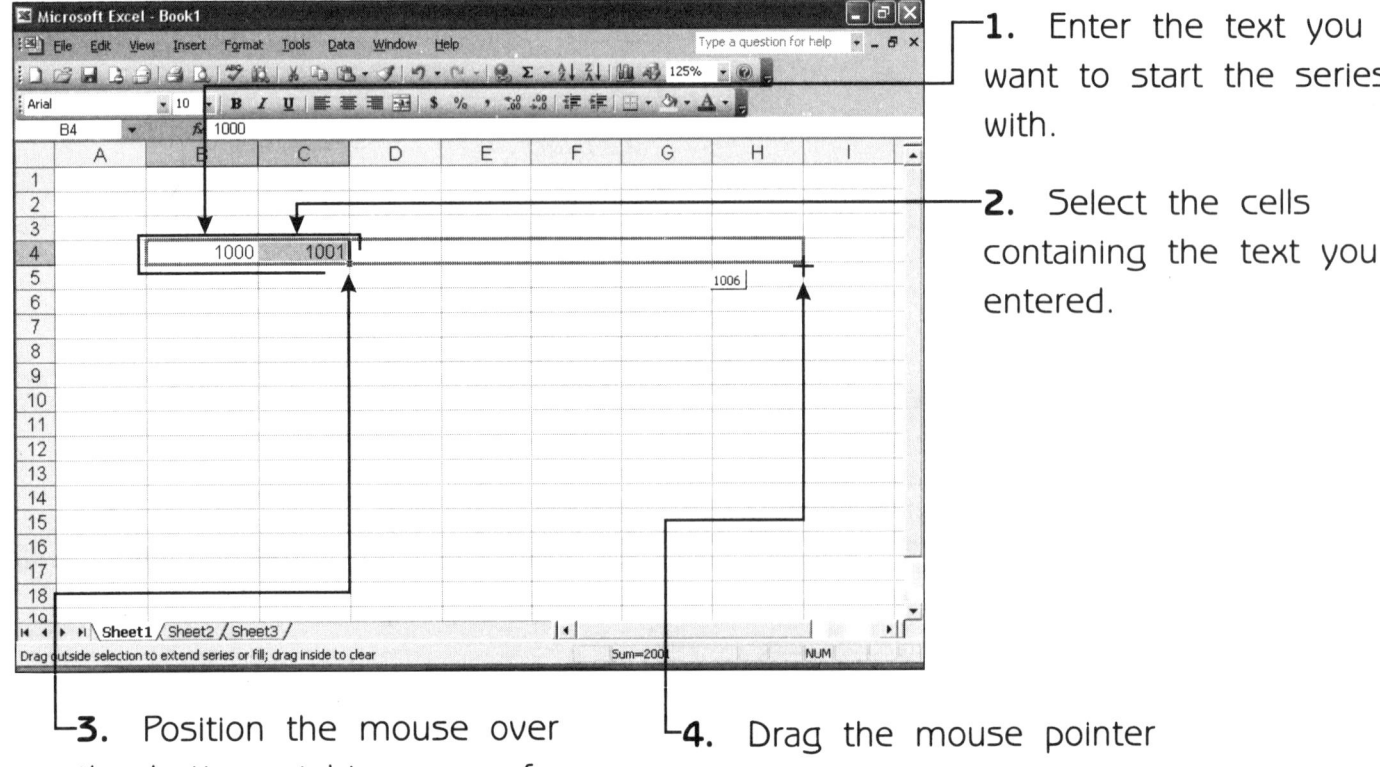

1. Enter the text you want to start the series with.

2. Select the cells containing the text you entered.

3. Position the mouse over the bottom right corner of the cell. The mouse pointer changes to [+].

4. Drag the mouse pointer over the cells you want to include in the series.

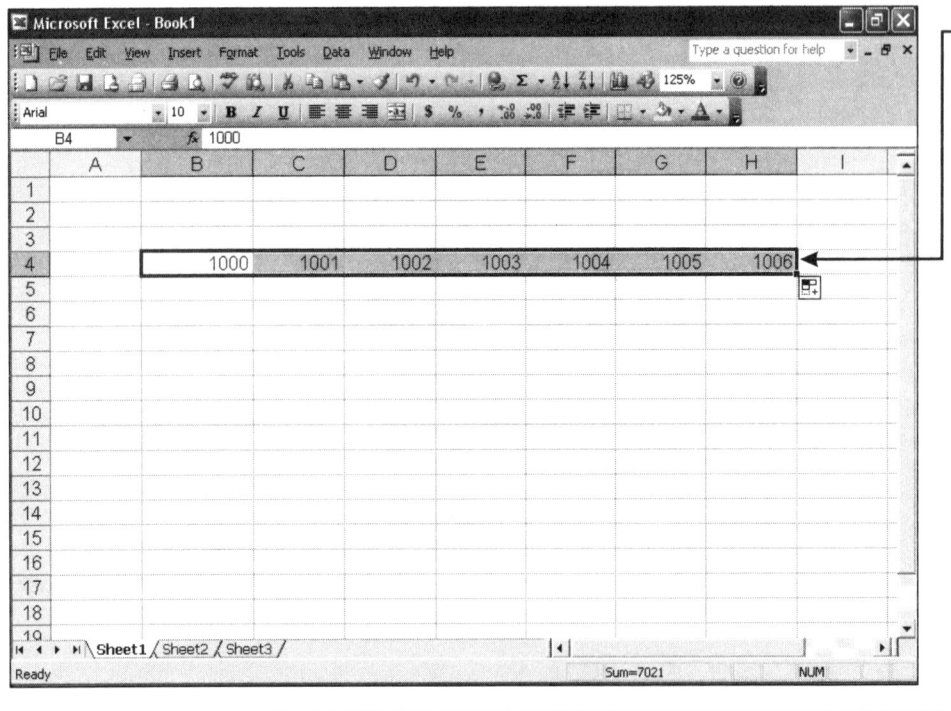

The cells display the number series. Click on any cell to deselect the cells.

Excel

Switching between Worksheets

You can switch to another worksheet in a workbook by clicking the tabs along the bottom of the document window. The sample workbook shown on the facing page actually has three available worksheets. You can create additional worksheets by choosing **Worksheet** from **Insert** menu.

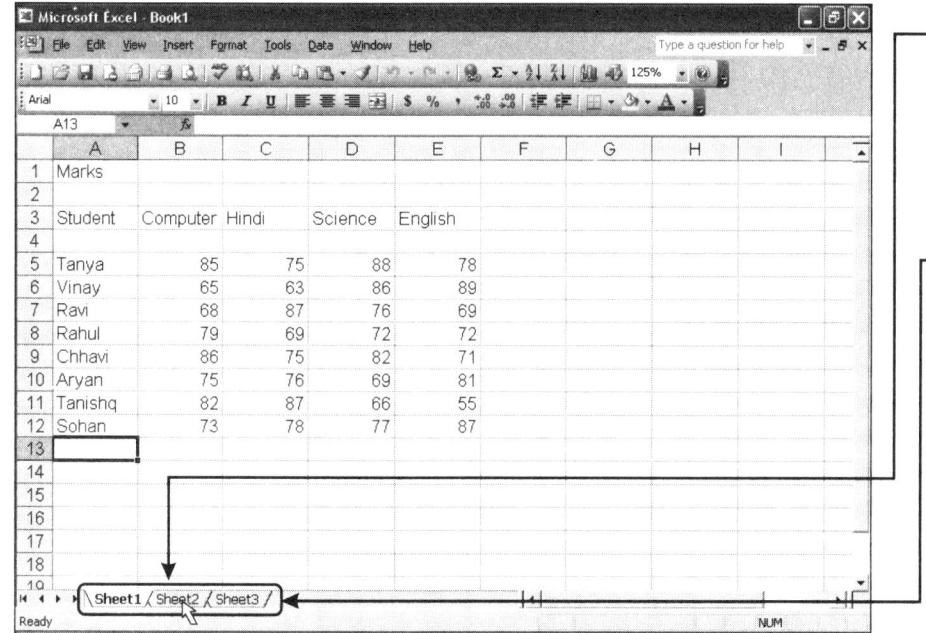

This area displays a tab for each worksheet in your workbook. The displayed worksheet has a white tab.

1. Click on the tab for the worksheet you want to display.

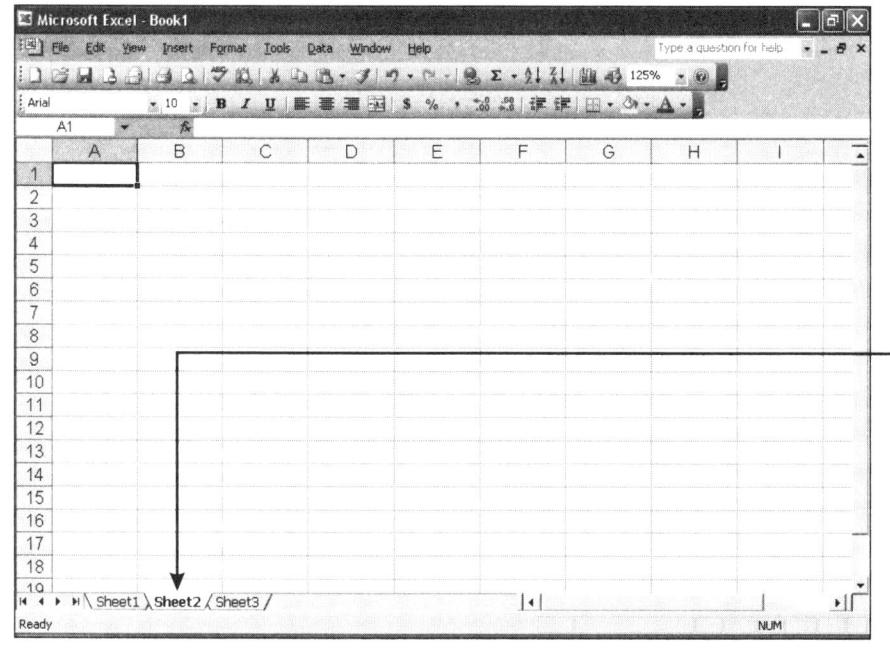

The selected worksheet appears.

The contents of the other worksheets in your workbook are hidden behind the displayed worksheet.

17

3. Save, Open and Edit the Worksheet

Saving a Workbook

You can save your workbook for future use. In the process of creating a workbook, if the computer is turned off or if there is a power failure, the workbook is lost. A saved workbook is referred to as a **file.** Saving a workbook allows you to review it later and make changes as and when required.

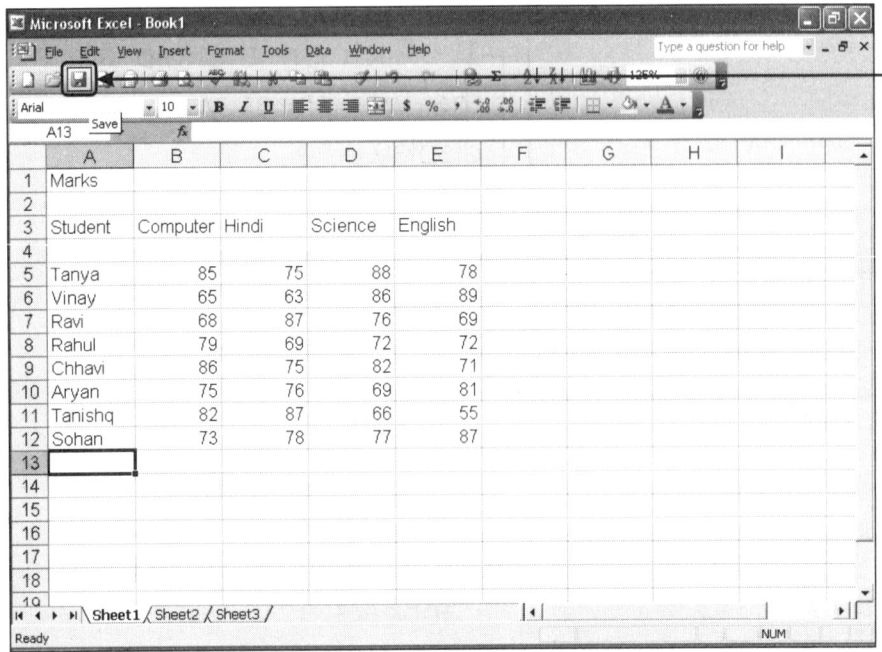

1. Click on the **Save** button (🖫) on the Standard toolbar to save your workbook.

The **Save As:** dialog box will appear.

*If you have previously saved your workbook, the **Save As:** dialog box will not appear since you have already named the workbook.*

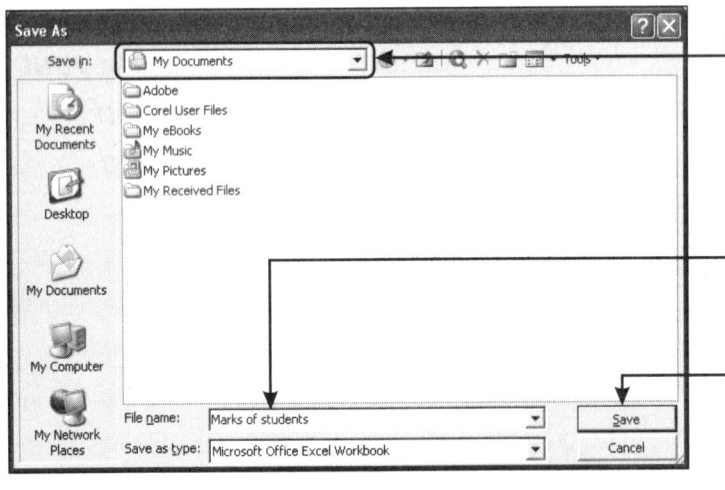

This area shows the location where Excel will store your workbook. You can click on this area to change the location.

2. Type a name for the workbook in the **File name:** text box.

3. Click on the **Save** button to save your workbook.

Excel will save your workbook.

18

Closing a Workbook

After you finish working on a workbook, you can close the workbook by clicking on the **Close** button at the right corner of the Menu bar. The workbook disappears from your screen.

Opening a Workbook

You can open a saved workbook to view the workbook on your screen. This allows you to review and make changes in the workbook.

1. Click on the **Open** button ( ) on the Standard toolbar to open a workbook. The **Open** dialog box appears.

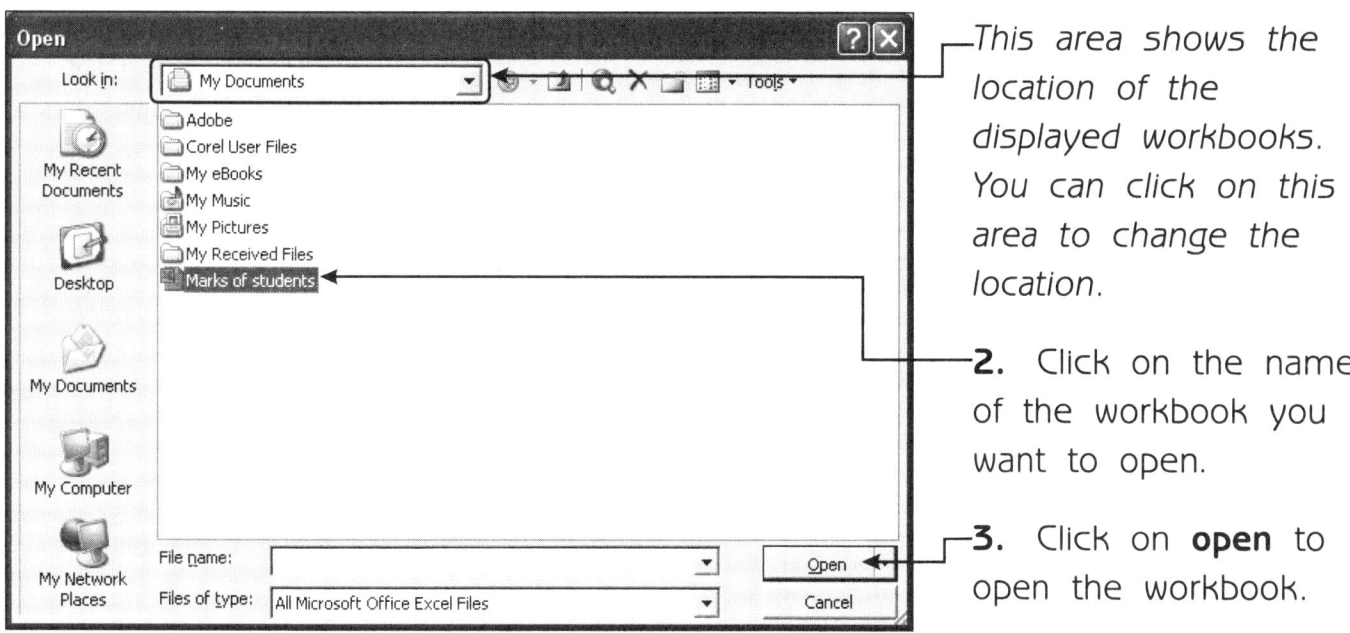

This area shows the location of the displayed workbooks. You can click on this area to change the location.

2. Click on the name of the workbook you want to open.

3. Click on **open** to open the workbook.

The workbook will open and appear on your screen.

The name of the open workbook will get displayed in the Title bar.

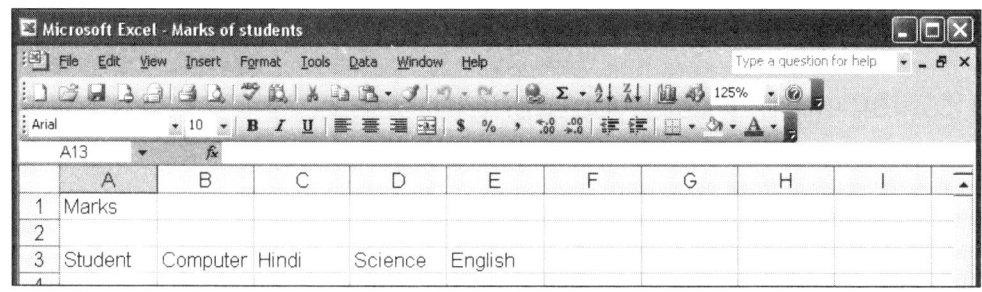

Drag and Drop Series

Editing Data

For correcting a mistake or updating data, you can edit the data in your worksheet.

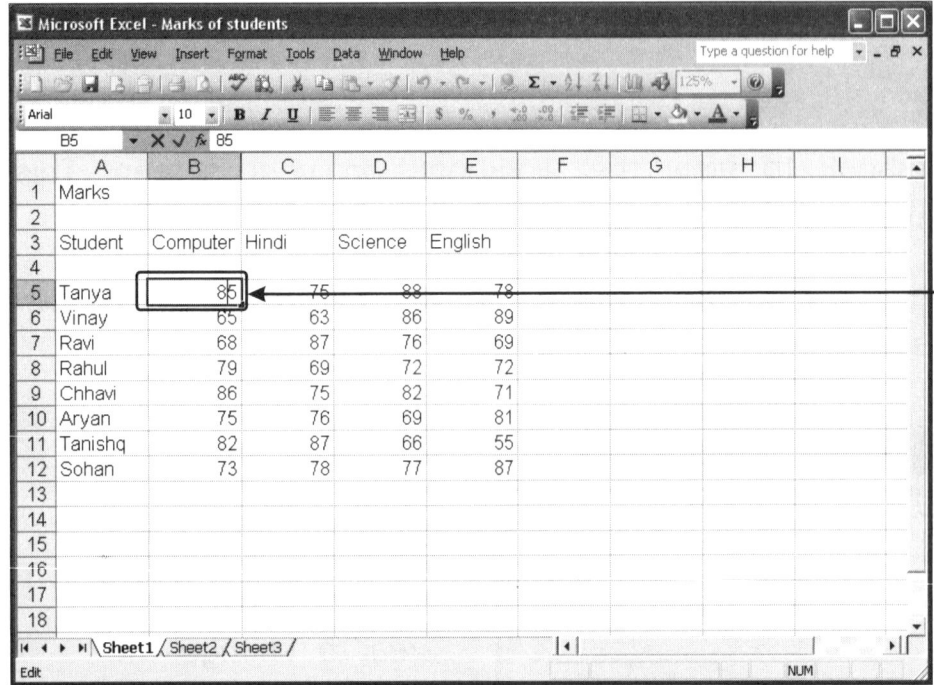

1. Double-click on the cell containing the data you want to edit.

A flashing insertion point appears in the cell.

2. Press the **arrow** keys on the keyboard to move the insertion point to where you want to remove or add characters.

3. To remove the character to the left of the flashing insertion point, press the **Backspace** key.

To remove the character to the right of the flashing insertion point, press the **Delete** *key.*

4. To add data where the insertion point flashes on your screen, type the data.

5. When you finish making changes to the data, press the **Enter** key.

Deleting Data

You can remove unnecessary data from the cells of your worksheet. You can delete data from a single cell or from several cells at once.

1. Select the cell or cells containing the data you want to delete.

2. Press the **Delete** key.

The data disappears from the cells you had selected.

20

Excel

Changing the Column Width

You can change the width of columns to improve the appearance of your worksheet and to display any hidden data.

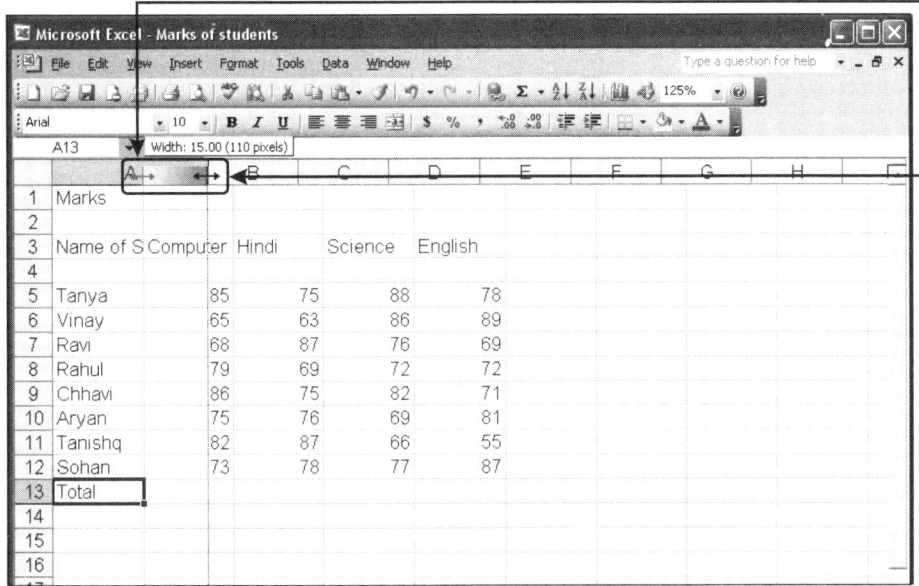

1. To change the width of a column, position the mouse (✥) over the right edge of the column heading. Mouse pointer changes to (↔).

2. Drag the column edge until the dotted line displays the column width you want.

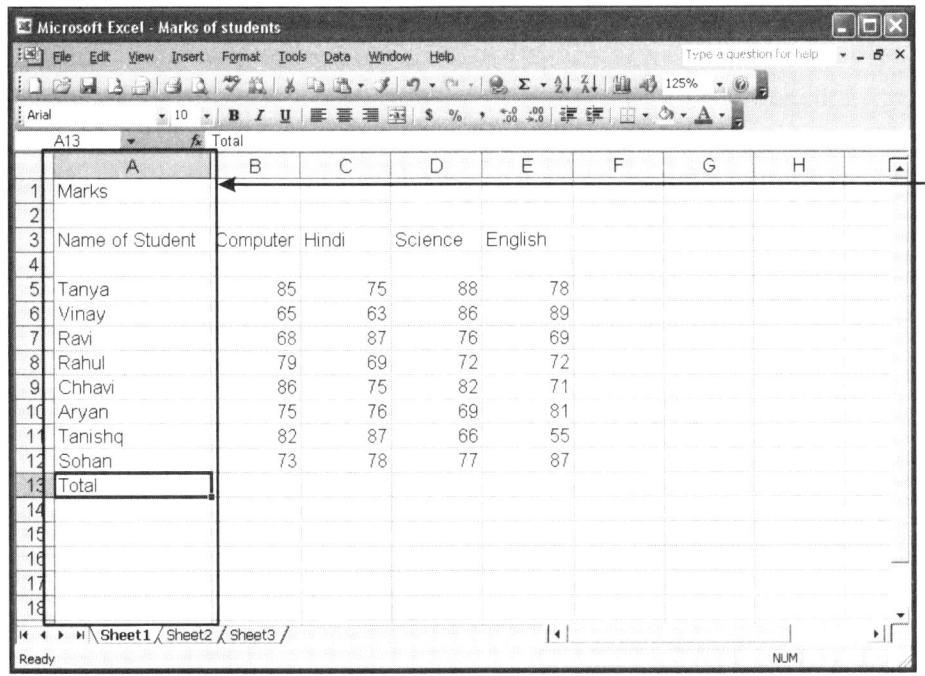

The column displays the new width.

To Fit the Longest Item

To change a column width to fit the longest item in the column, double-click on the right edge of the column heading.

21

Drag and Drop Series

Changing the Row Height

You can change the height of rows to add space between the rows of data in your worksheet.

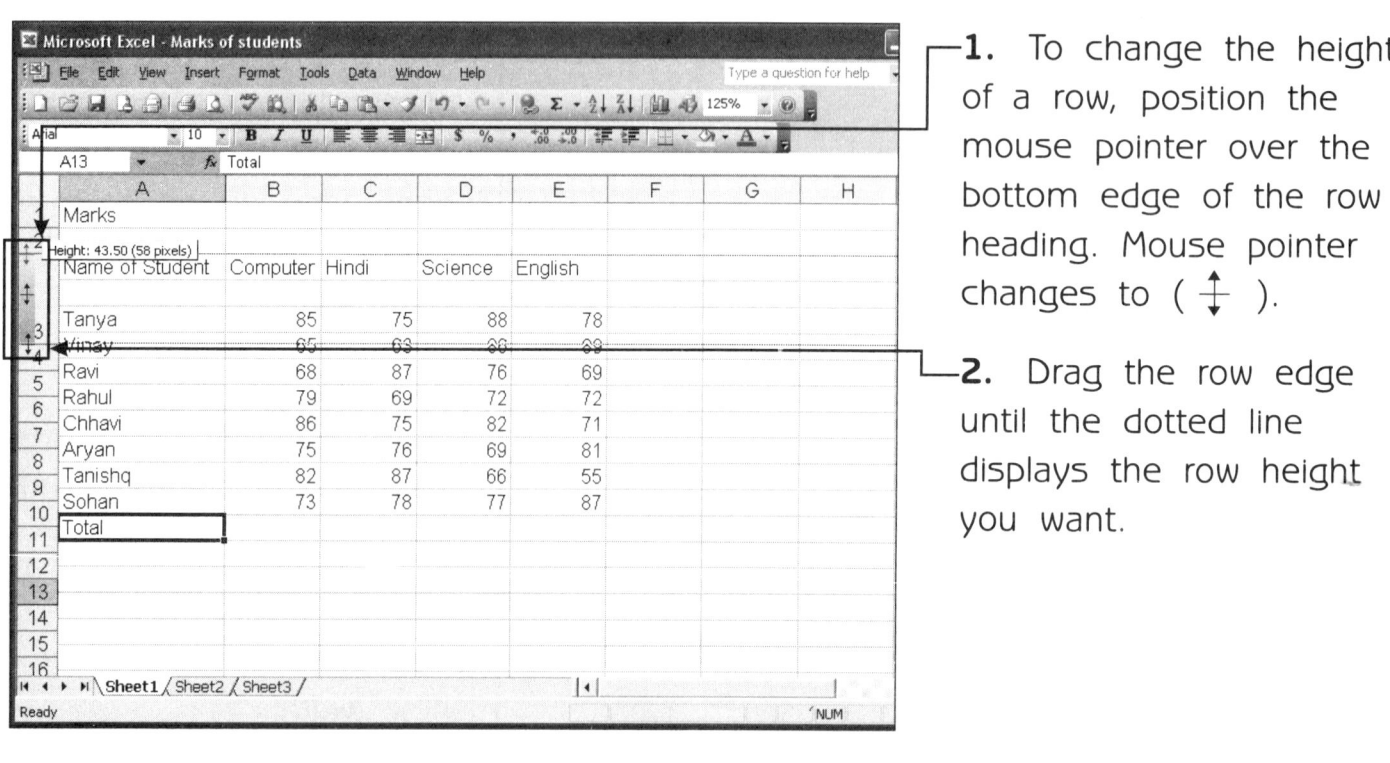

1. To change the height of a row, position the mouse pointer over the bottom edge of the row heading. Mouse pointer changes to (⇕).

2. Drag the row edge until the dotted line displays the row height you want.

The row displays the new height.

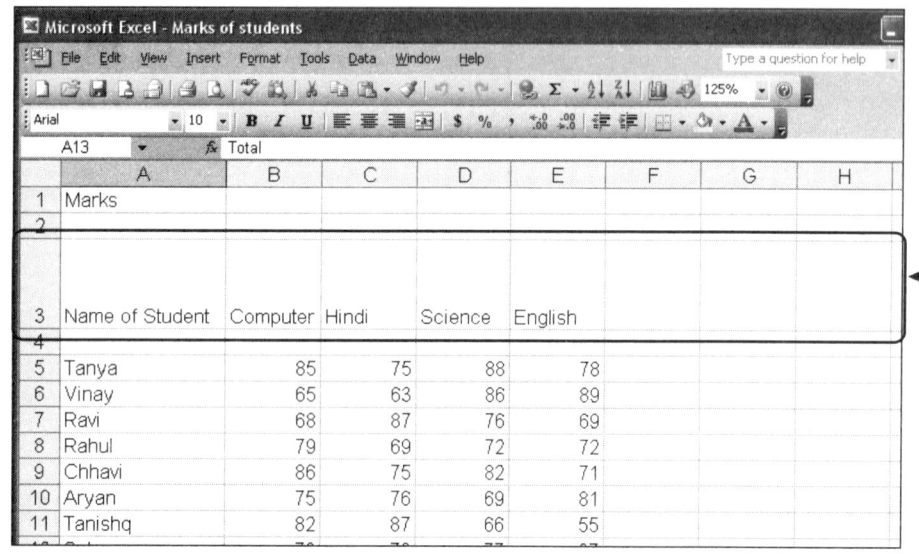

To Fit the Tallest Item

To change a row height to fit the tallest item in the row, double-click on the bottom edge of row heading.

Excel

Inserting a Row

You can add a row to your worksheet to insert additional data.

To insert a row above the row you select.

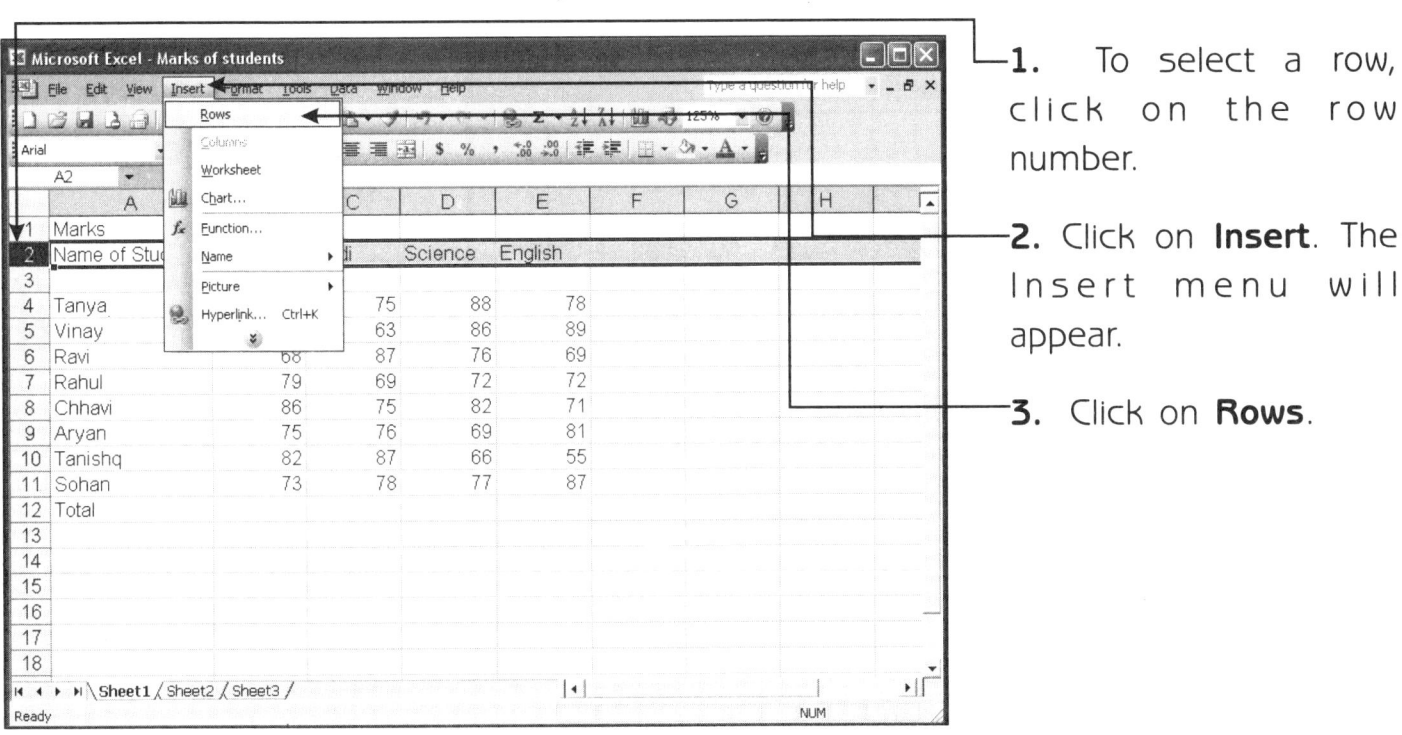

1. To select a row, click on the row number.

2. Click on **Insert**. The Insert menu will appear.

3. Click on **Rows**.

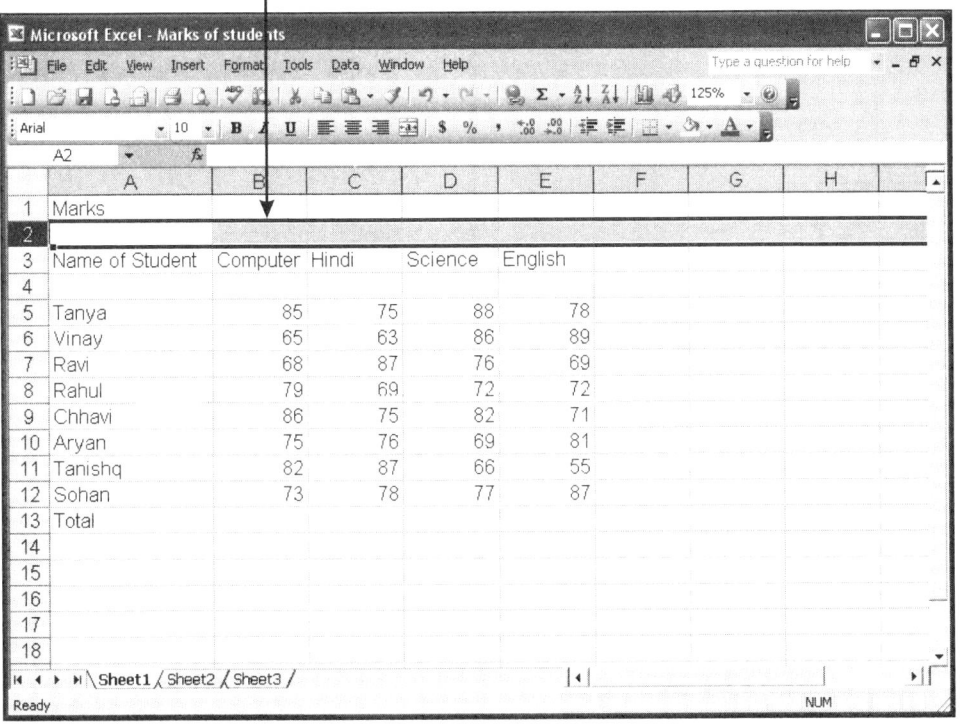

The new row appears and all the rows that follow, shift downward.

To deselect a row, click on any cell.

23

Drag and Drop Series

Inserting a Column

You can add a column to your worksheet to insert additional data.

To insert a column to the left of the column you select.

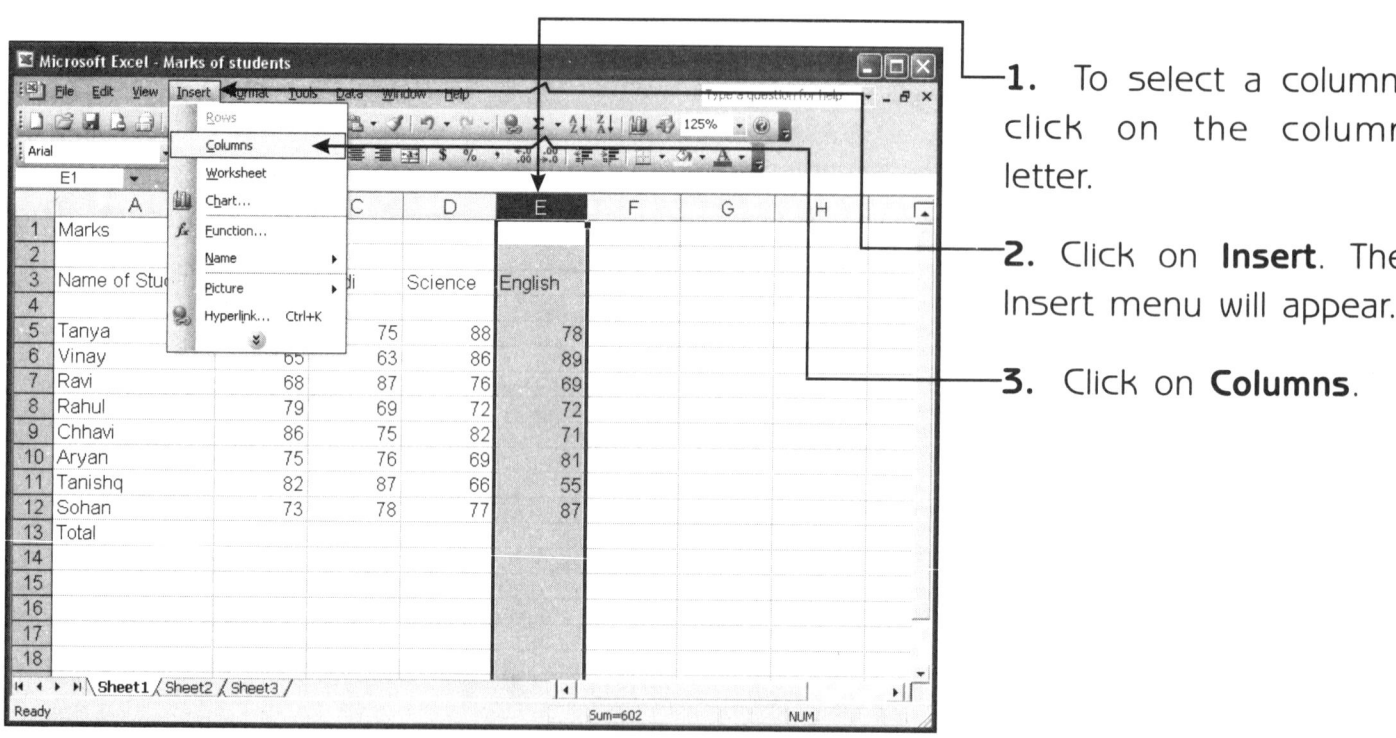

1. To select a column, click on the column letter.

2. Click on **Insert**. The Insert menu will appear.

3. Click on **Columns**.

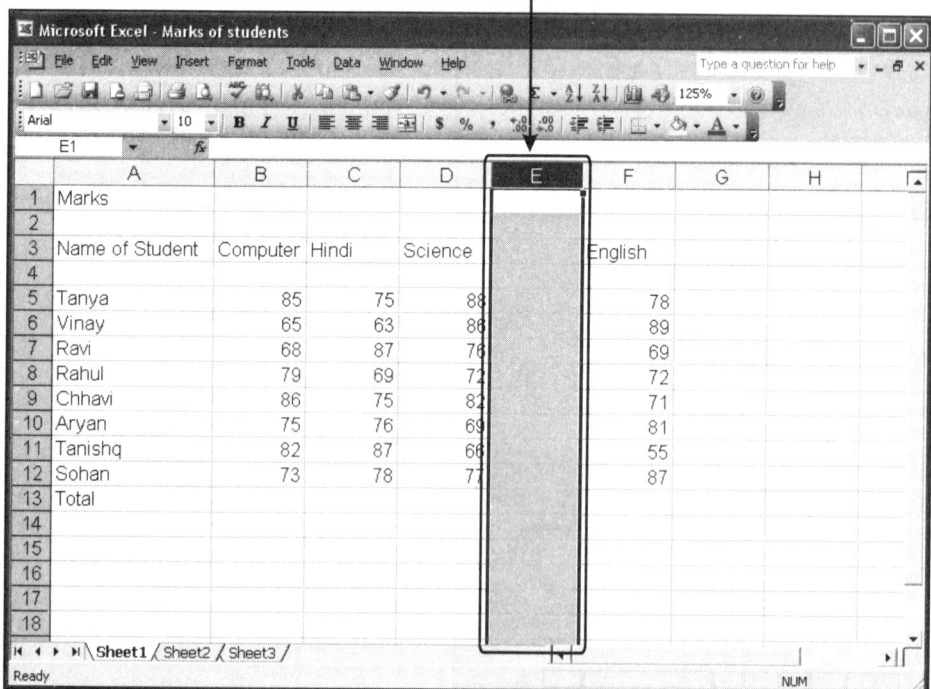

The new column appears and all the columns that follow, shift to the right.

To deselect a column, click on any cell.

4. Formula and Function

Formula

The expressions which help you to calculate and analyze the data in your worksheet are known as **formulae**. A formula in the worksheet always begins with an equal sign (=).

Operators

A formula is a Mathematical expression which contains one or more operators. The type of calculation you want to perform is specified by an **operator**. Arithmetic operator and Comparison operator are the two types of operator.

Arithmetic Operator

Arithmetic operators are used to perform mathematical calculations. Some of the most commonly used arithmetic operators are + (addition), — (Subtraction), * (multiplication), / (Division), % (Percent) and, ^ (Exponentiation).

Comparison Operator

Comparison operators are used to compare two values. Comparison operators return a value of TRUE or FALSE.

Some of the Comparison operators are: = (Equal to), > (Greater than), < (Less than), >= (Greater than or equal to), <= (Less than or equal to), <> (Not equal to).

Cell Reference

It is convenient to use **cell reference** instead of actual data at the time of working with formulae. For example, enter the formula =A1+A2 instead of =100+200.

When you use cell reference and you change a number used in a formula, Excel will automatically redo the calculation for you.

Drag and Drop Series

Functions

A ready-to-use formula that you can use to perform a calculation on the data in your worksheet is referred to as **function**. AVERAGE, COUNT, SUM and MAX are some common functions.

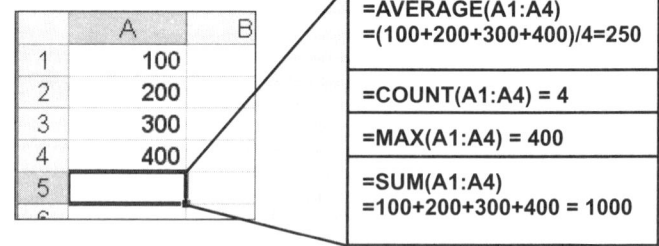

Entering a Formula

A formula helps you to calculate and analyze data in your worksheet and can be entered in any cell.

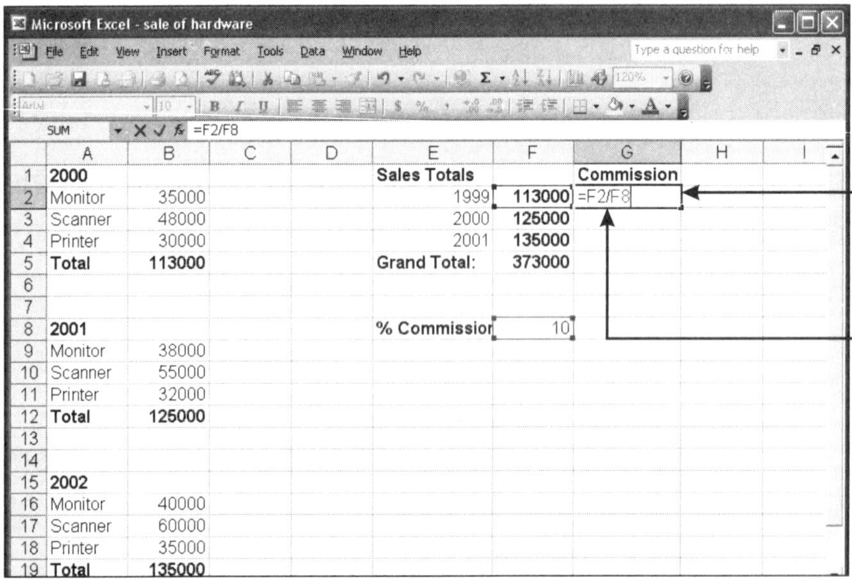

1. Click on the cell where you want to enter a formula.

2. Type in an equal to sign (=) to begin the formula.

3. Type the formula and then press the **Enter** key.

The result of the calculation appears in the cell.

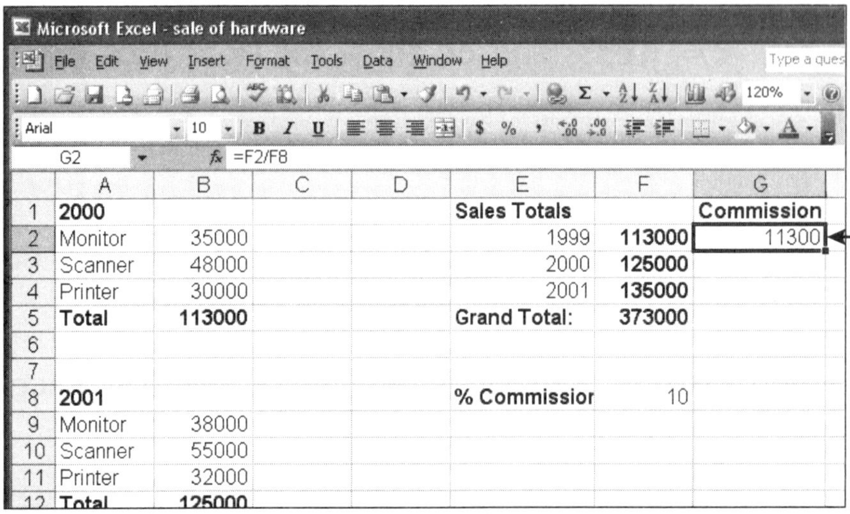

4. To view the formula you entered, click on the cell containing the formula. The formula bar displays the formula for the cell.

26

Excel

Editing a Formula

You can also edit the formula in your worksheet.

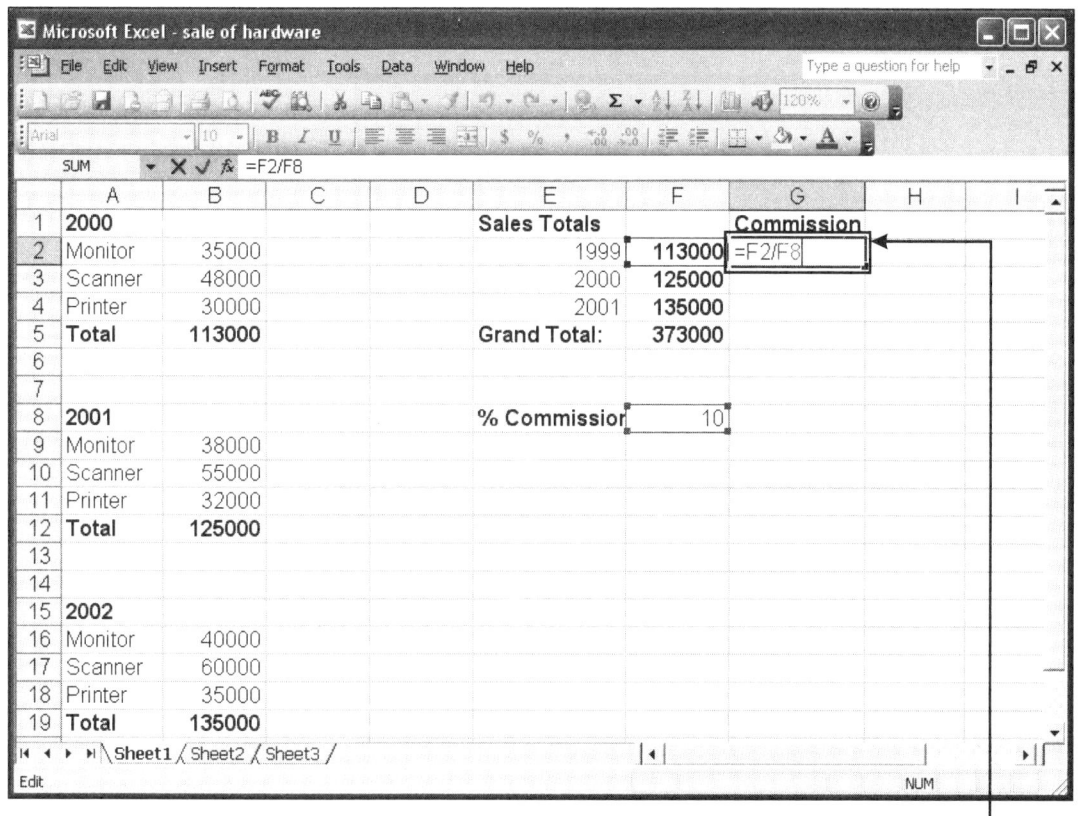

1. Double-click on the cell containing the formula you want to change.

The formula appears in the cell. Excel outlines each cell used in the formula with a different color.

2. Press the **arrow** key on the keyboard to move the flashing insertion point to where you want to remove or add characters.

3. Type the data where the insertion point flashes on your screen.

4. When you finish making the changes to the formula, press the **Enter** key.

Drag and Drop Series

Entering a Function

Excel helps you enter functions into your worksheet. These functions allow you to perform calculations without typing long, complex formulae.

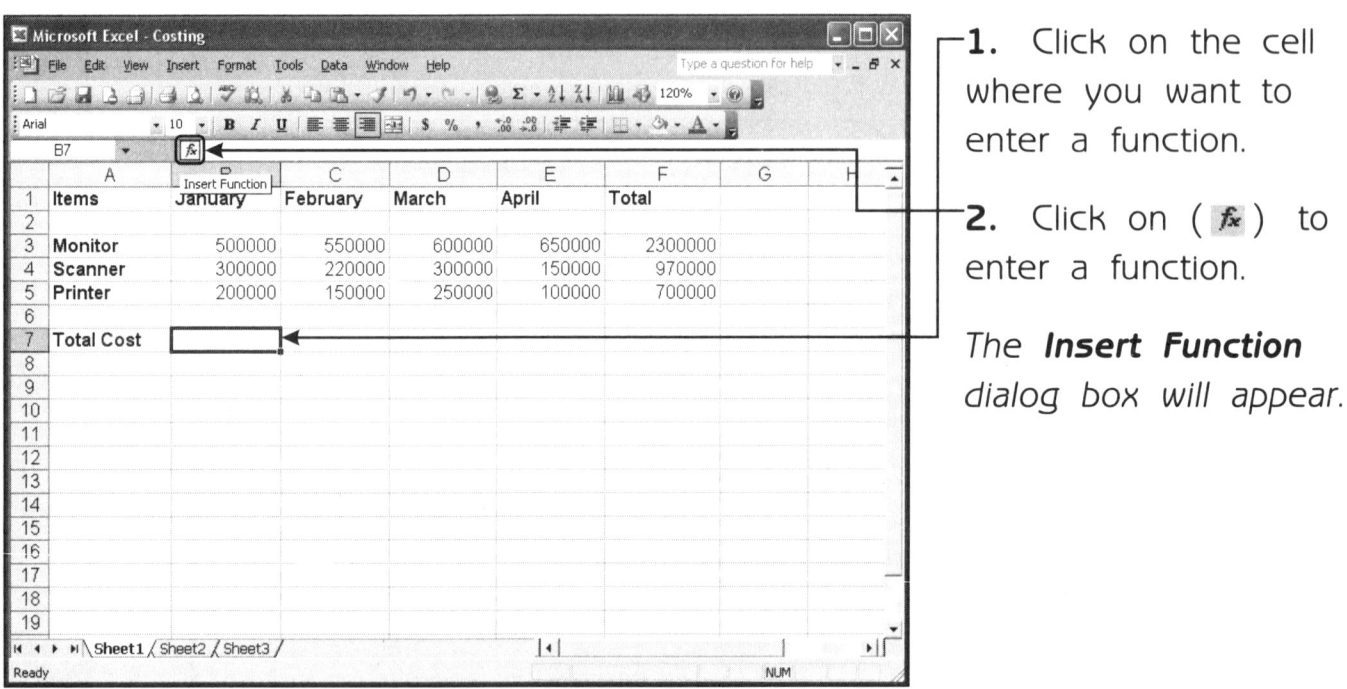

1. Click on the cell where you want to enter a function.

2. Click on (*fx*) to enter a function.

*The **Insert Function** dialog box will appear.*

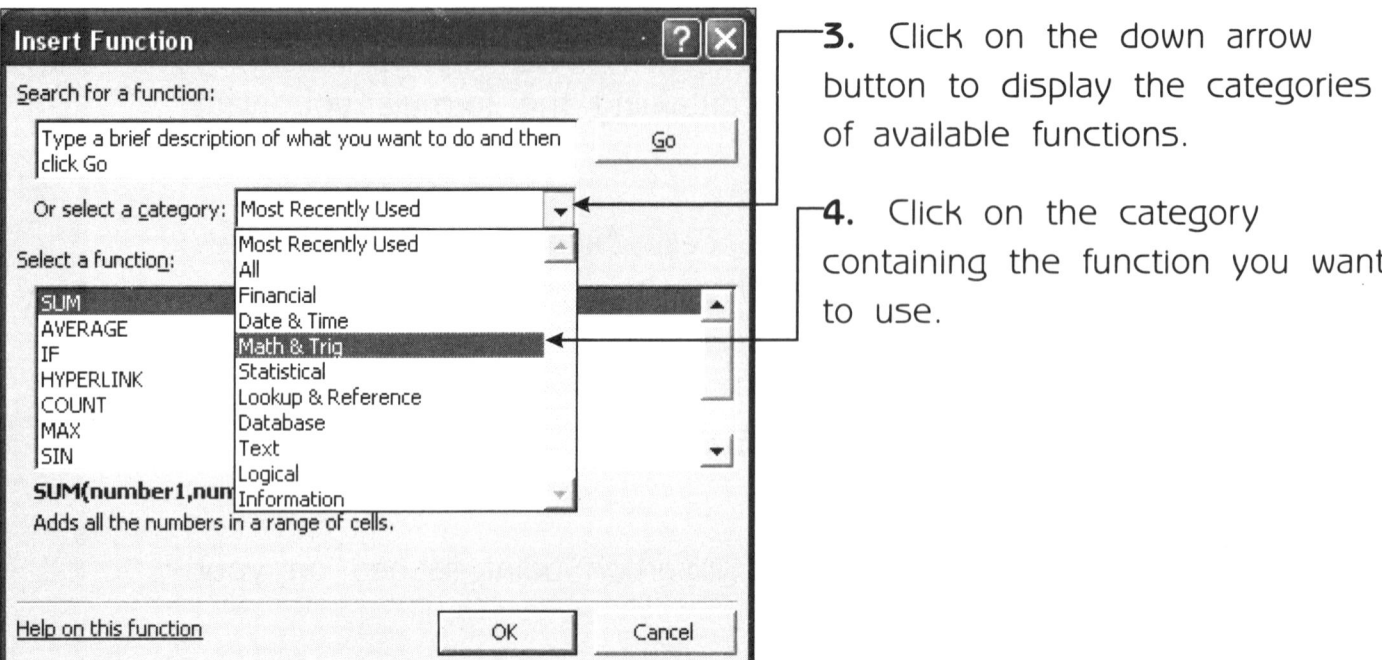

3. Click on the down arrow button to display the categories of available functions.

4. Click on the category containing the function you want to use.

*If you do not know which category contains the function, select **All** from the list to display a list of all the functions.*

Excel

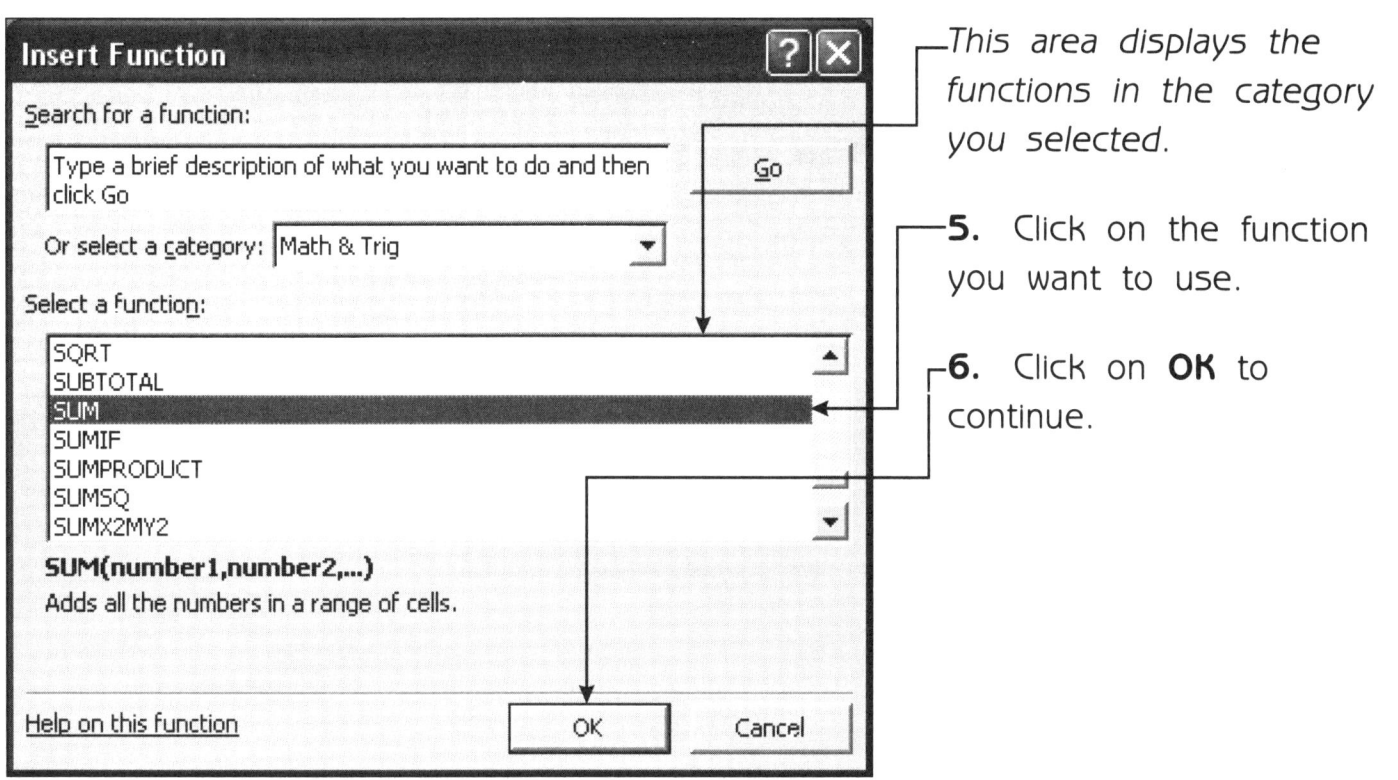

This area displays the functions in the category you selected.

5. Click on the function you want to use.

6. Click on **OK** to continue.

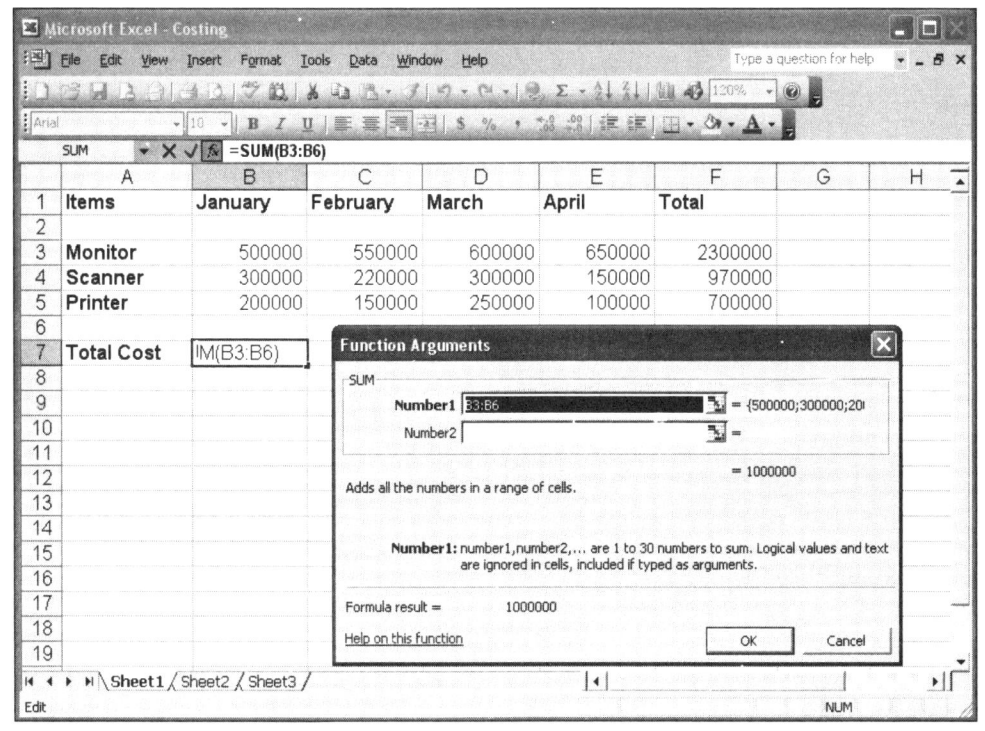

The **Function Arguments** dialog box appears.

If the dialog box covers data you want to use in the calculation, you can move the dialog box to a new location.

Drag and Drop Series

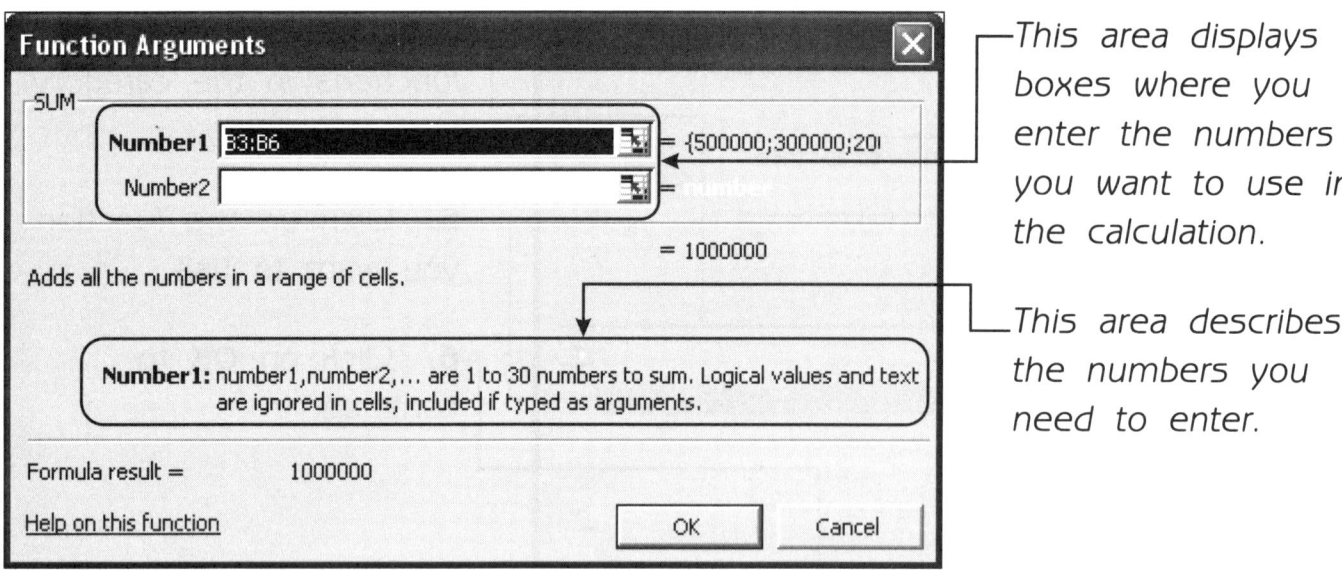

This area displays boxes where you enter the numbers you want to use in the calculation.

This area describes the numbers you need to enter.

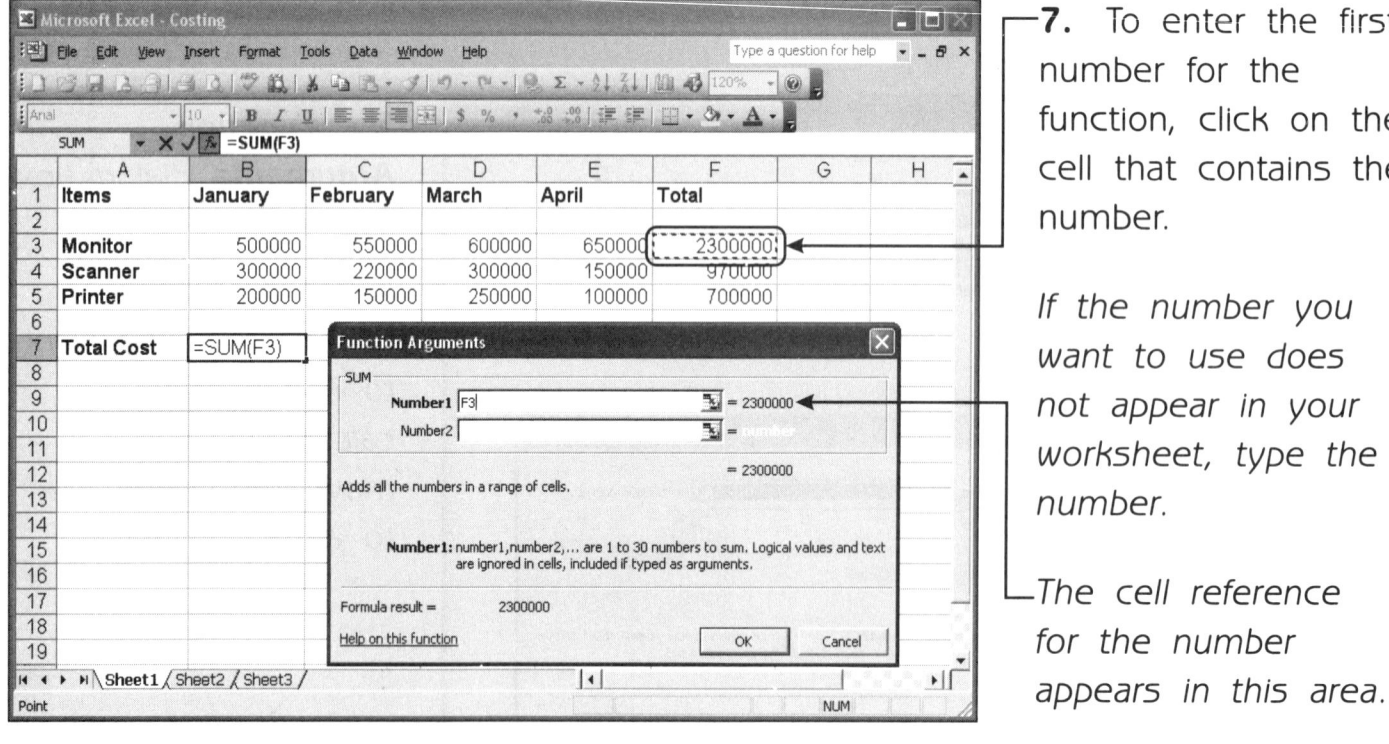

7. To enter the first number for the function, click on the cell that contains the number.

If the number you want to use does not appear in your worksheet, type the number.

The cell reference for the number appears in this area.

Excel

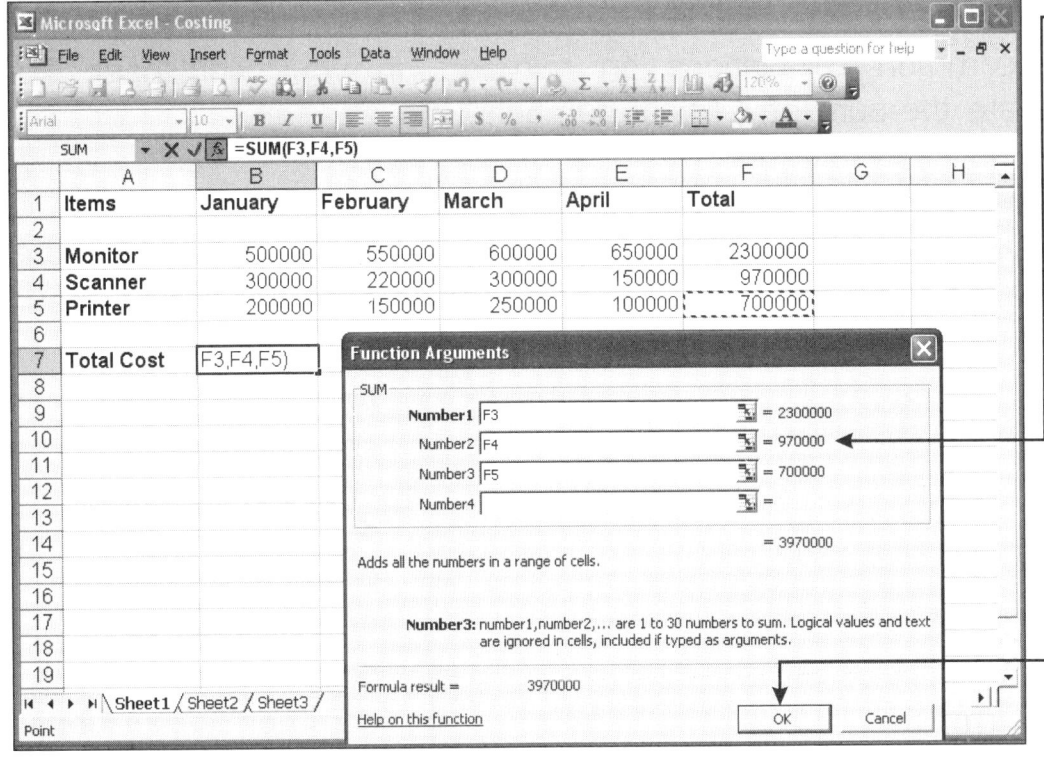

8. Click on the next box to enter the next number.

9. Repeat steps 7 and 8 until you have entered all the numbers you want to use in the calculation.

10. Click on the **OK** button to enter the function into your worksheet.

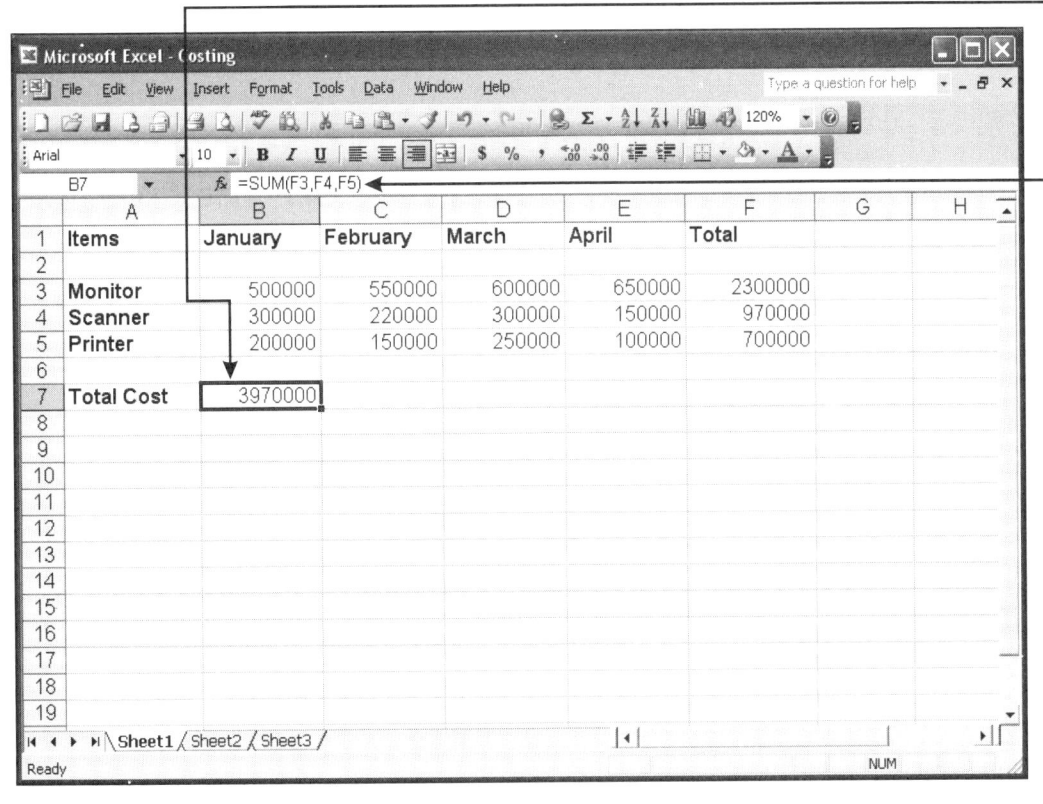

The result of the function appears in the cell.

The Formula bar displays the function for the cell.

31

Drag and Drop Series

Common Calculation

You can make quick common calculations on numbers in your worksheet. For example, you can calculate the sum of a list of numbers.

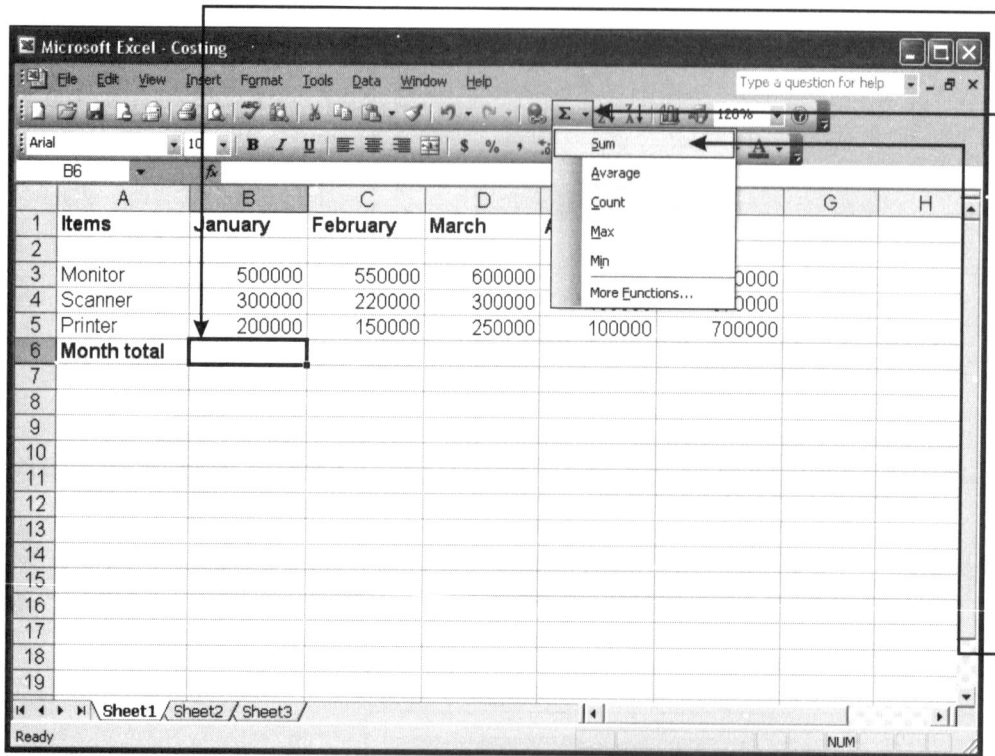

1. Click the cell below or right of the cells containing the numbers you want to include in the calculation.

2. Click on the down arrow button of this area to display a list of common calculations.

3. Click on the calculation you want to perform.

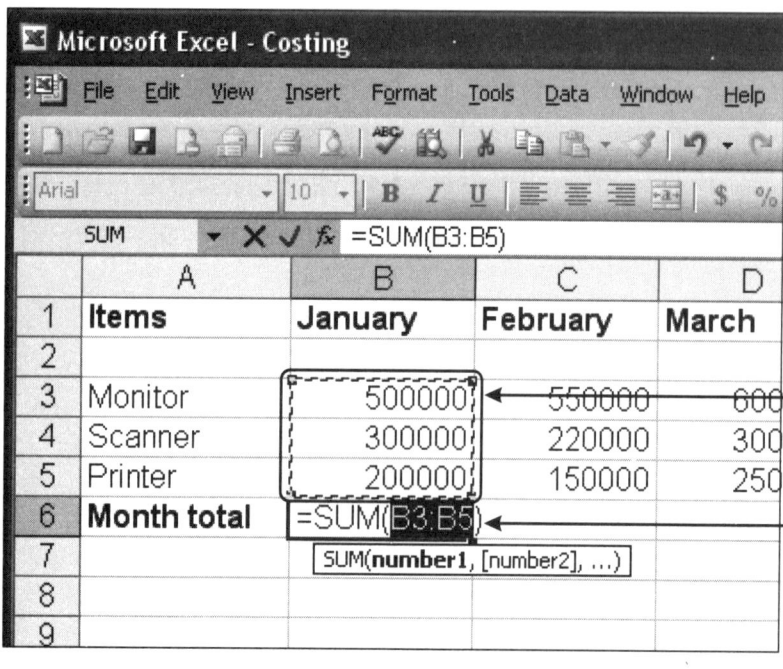

A moving outline appears around the cells that Excel will include in the calculation.

If Excel outlines the wrong cells, you can select the cells that contain the numbers you want to include in the calculation.

The cell you selected in step 1 displays the function Excel will use to perform the calculation.

Excel

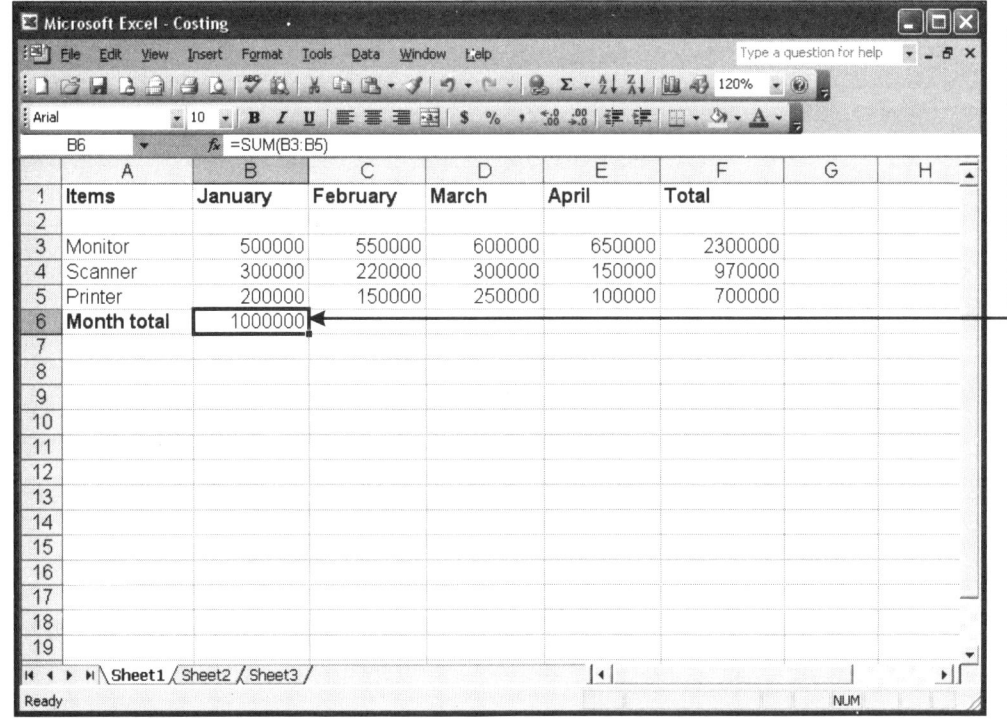

4. Press the **Enter** key on the keyboard to perform the calculation.

To Add Numbers Quickly

You can quickly display the sum of a list of numbers without entering a formula into your worksheet.

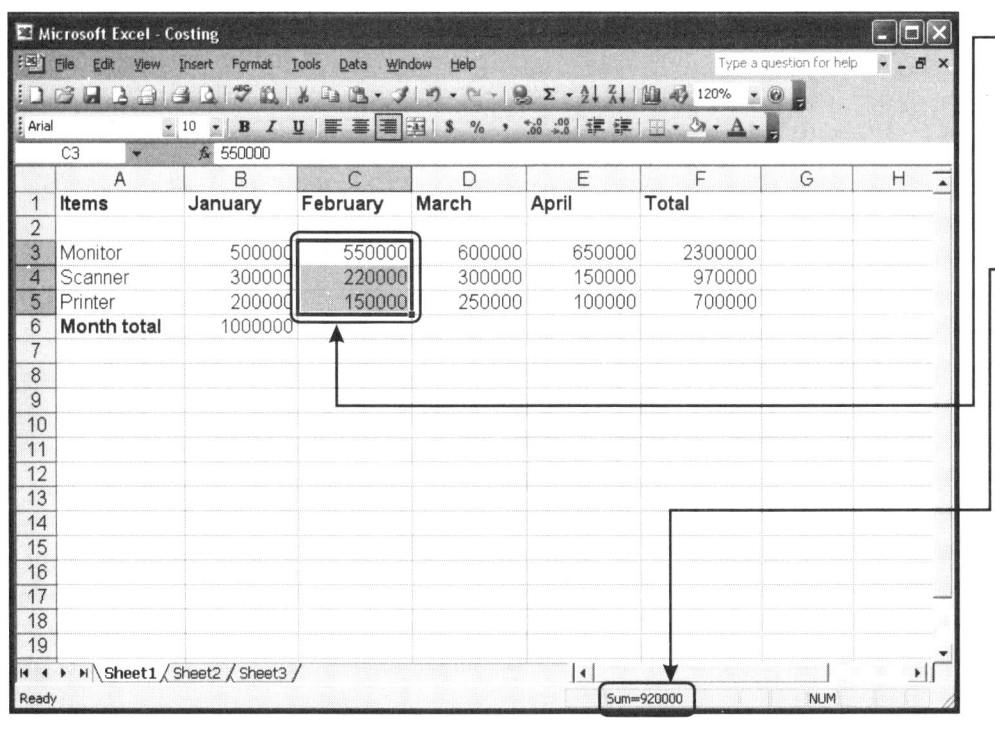

1. Select the cells containing the numbers you want to add.

This area displays the sum of the cells you had selected.

33

5. Formatting the Worksheet

Changing the Font of Data

You can change the font of your data to enhance the appearance of your worksheet.

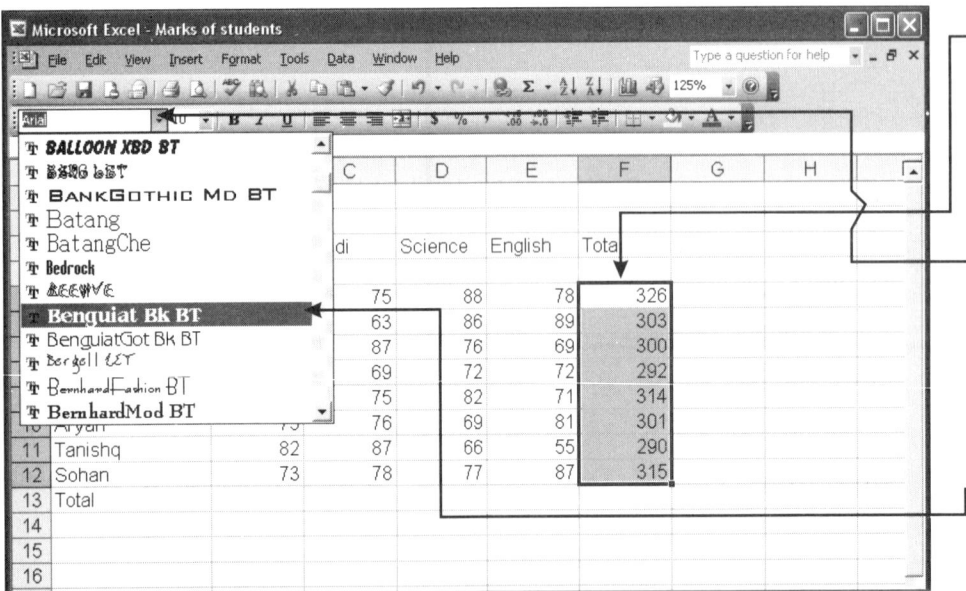

1. Select the cells containing the data you want to change to a different font.

2. Click on the down arrow button of Font to display a list of the available fonts.

3. Click on the font you want to use.

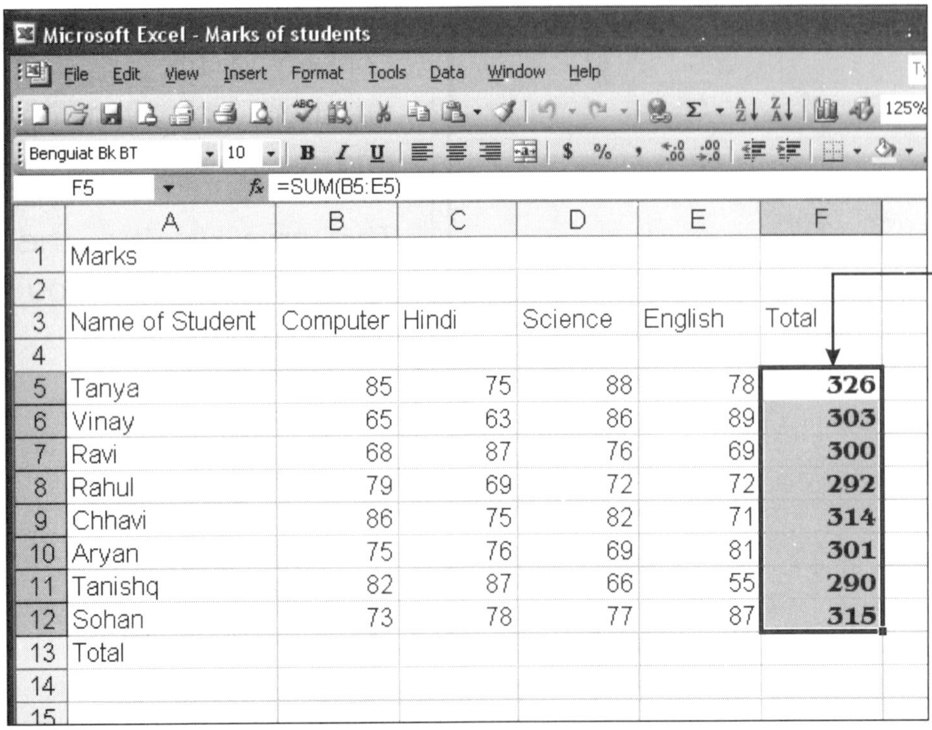

The data changes to the font you selected.

To deselect the cells, click on any cell.

34

Changing the Size of Data

You can increase or decrease the size of the data in your worksheet.

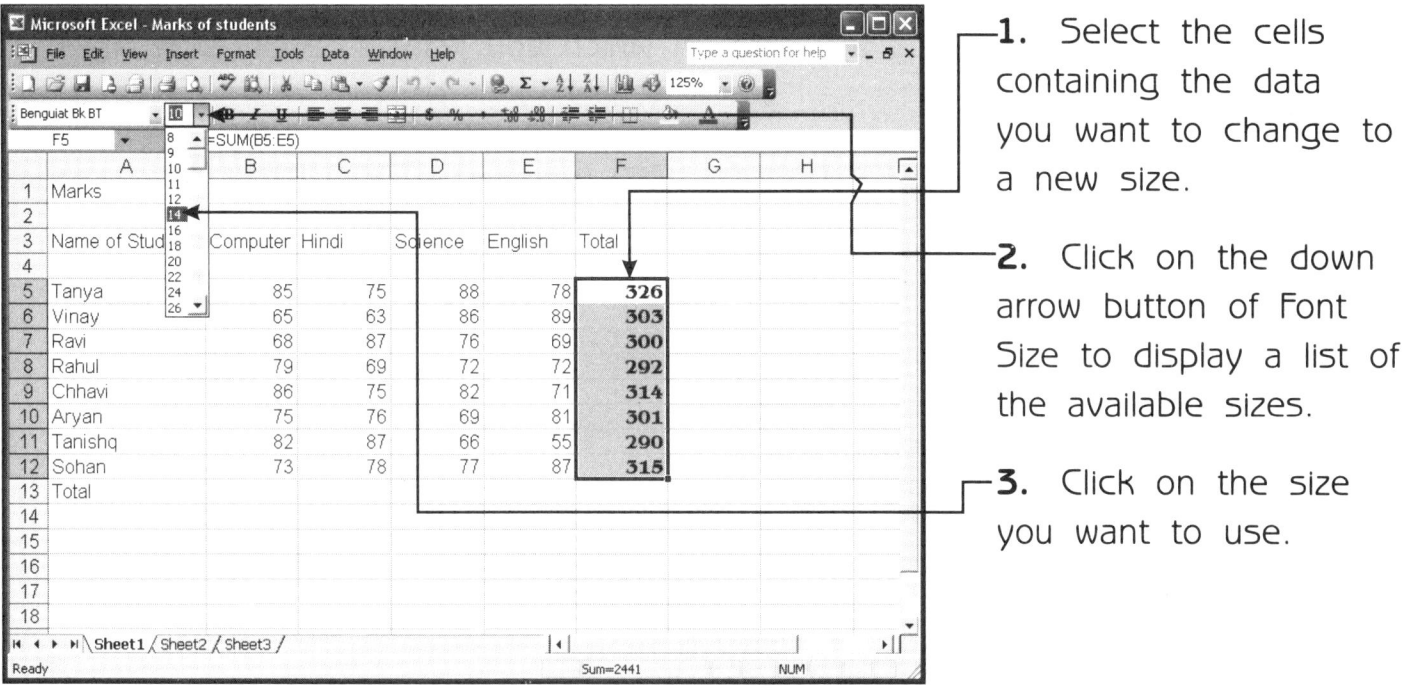

1. Select the cells containing the data you want to change to a new size.

2. Click on the down arrow button of Font Size to display a list of the available sizes.

3. Click on the size you want to use.

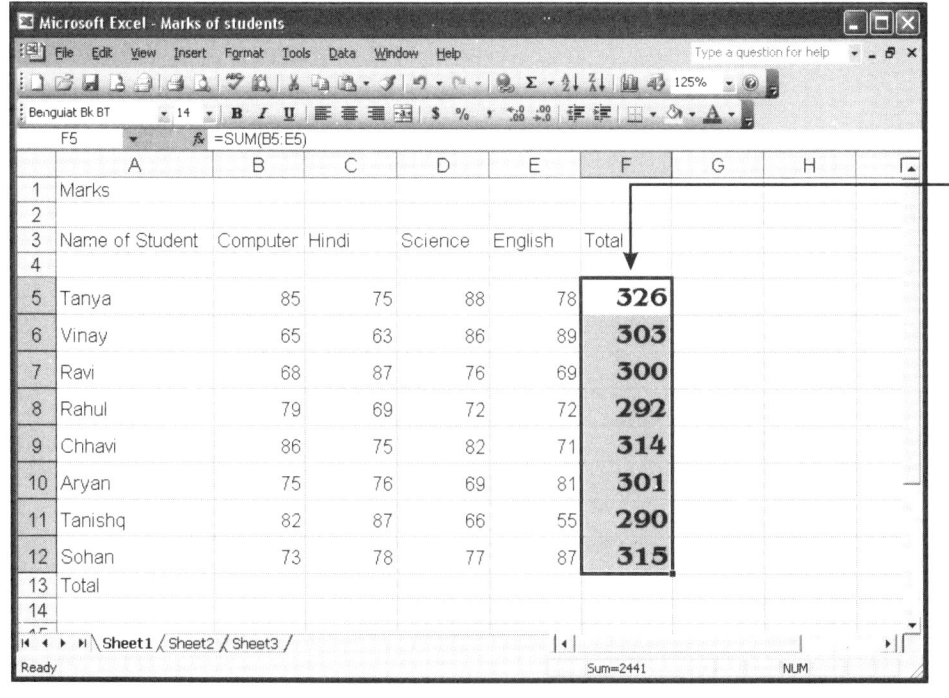

The data changes to the size you selected.

To deselect the cells, click on any cell.

Drag and Drop Series

Bold, Italic and Underline

You can make the data bold or italic, or underline it in your worksheet.

1. Select the cells containing the data on which you want to apply bold, italic or underline.

2. Click on one of the following buttons from the Formatting toolbar:

(**B**) Bold

(*I*) Italic

(U) Underline

The data will appear in the style you have selected.

To remove a bold, italic or underline style, repeat steps 1 and 2.

Changing the Alignment of Data

You can align data in different ways to enhance the appearance of your worksheet.

1. Select the cells containing the data you want to align in a different style.

2. Click on one of the following buttons from the Formatting toolbar:

(≡) Left align

(≡) Center

(≡) Right align

The data will appear in the new alignment.

To deselect the cells, click on any cell.

6. Working with Charts

Creating a Chart

Charts allow you to easily compare data and view patterns and trends.

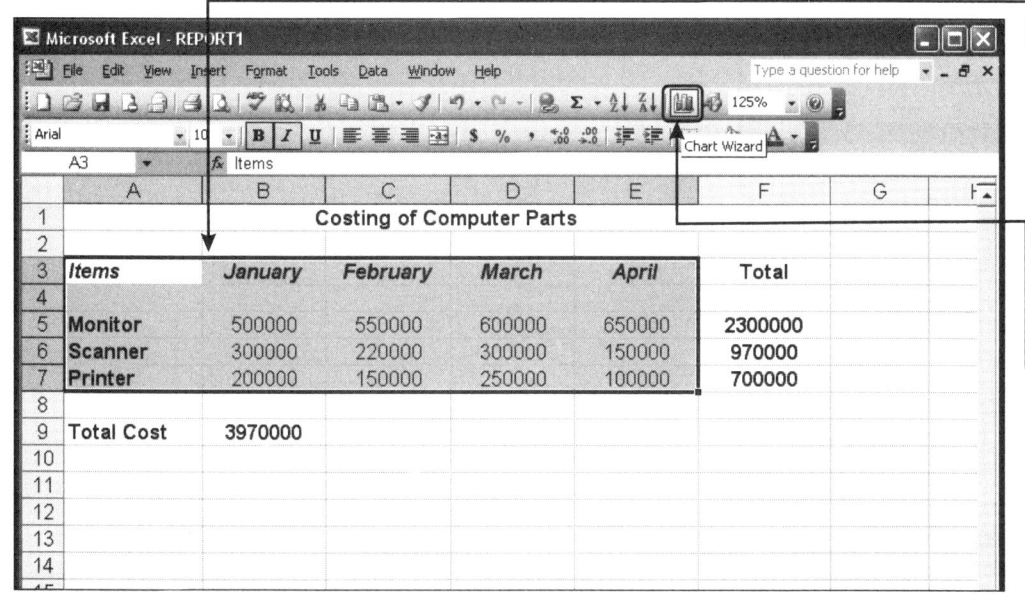

1. Select the cells containing the data you want to display in a chart, including the row and column labels.

2. Click on **Charts Wizard** (📊) to create a chart.

*The **Chart Wizard** window appears.*

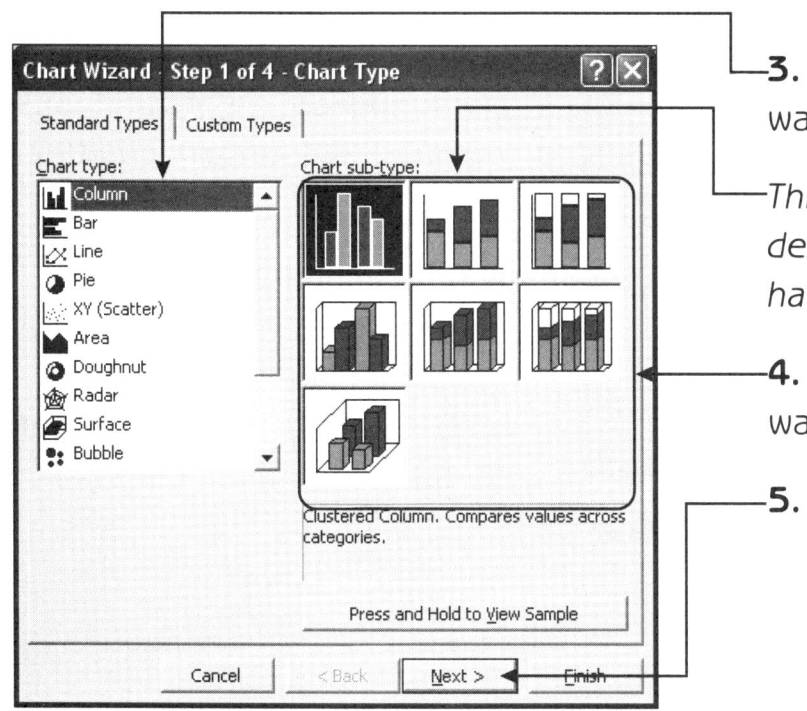

3. Click on the type of chart you want to create.

This area displays the available chart designs for the type of chart you have selected.

4. Click on any chart design you want to use.

5. Click on **Next** to continue.

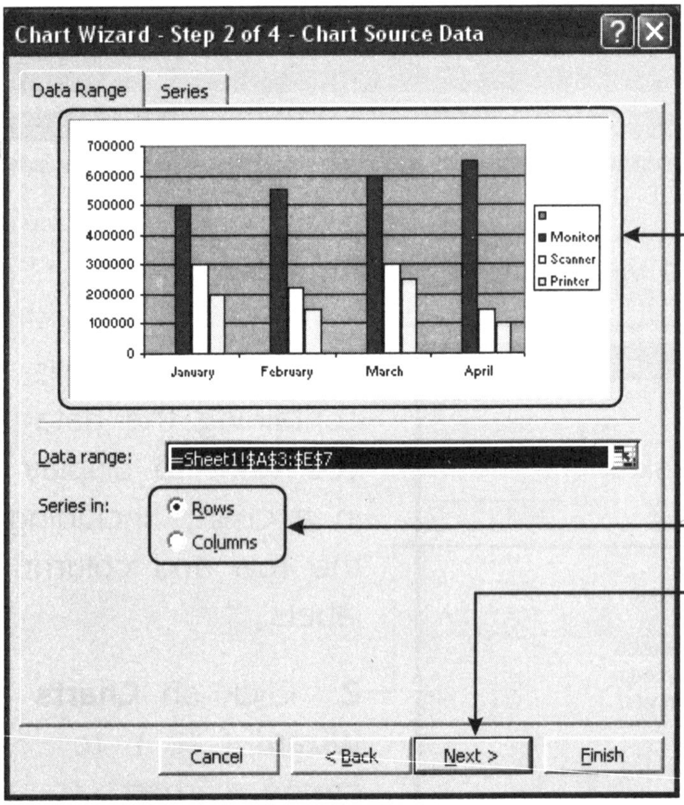

Drag and Drop Series

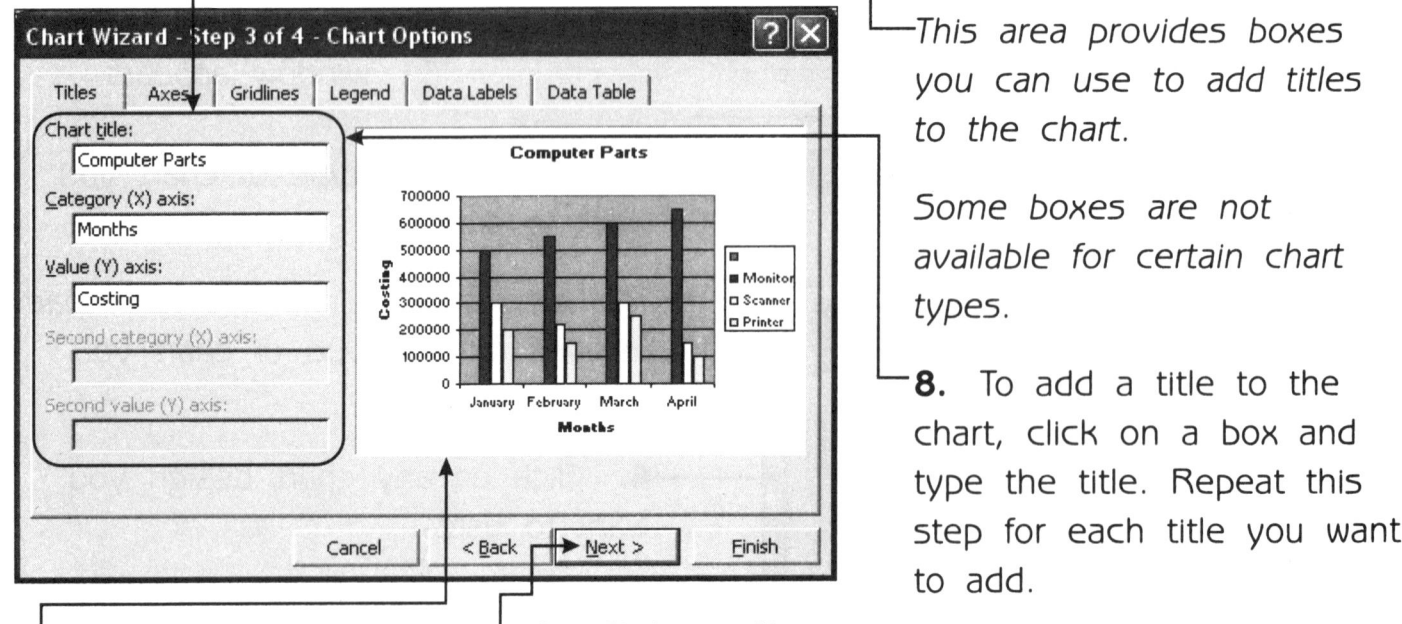

6. Click on the radio button of an option to specify the way you want Excel to plot the data from your worksheet.

This area displays a preview of the chart.

7. Click on **Next** to continue.

This area provides boxes you can use to add titles to the chart.

Some boxes are not available for certain chart types.

8. To add a title to the chart, click on a box and type the title. Repeat this step for each title you want to add.

This area shows how the titles will appear in the chart.

9. Click on **Next** to continue.

Excel

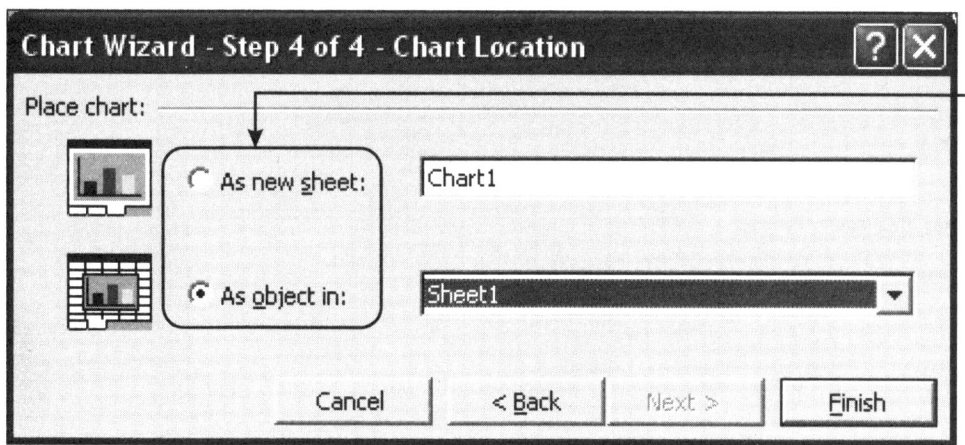

10. Click on the radio button of an option to specify where you want to display the chart.

As new sheet: displays the chart on its own sheet, called a chart sheet.

As object in: displays the chart on the same worksheet as the data.

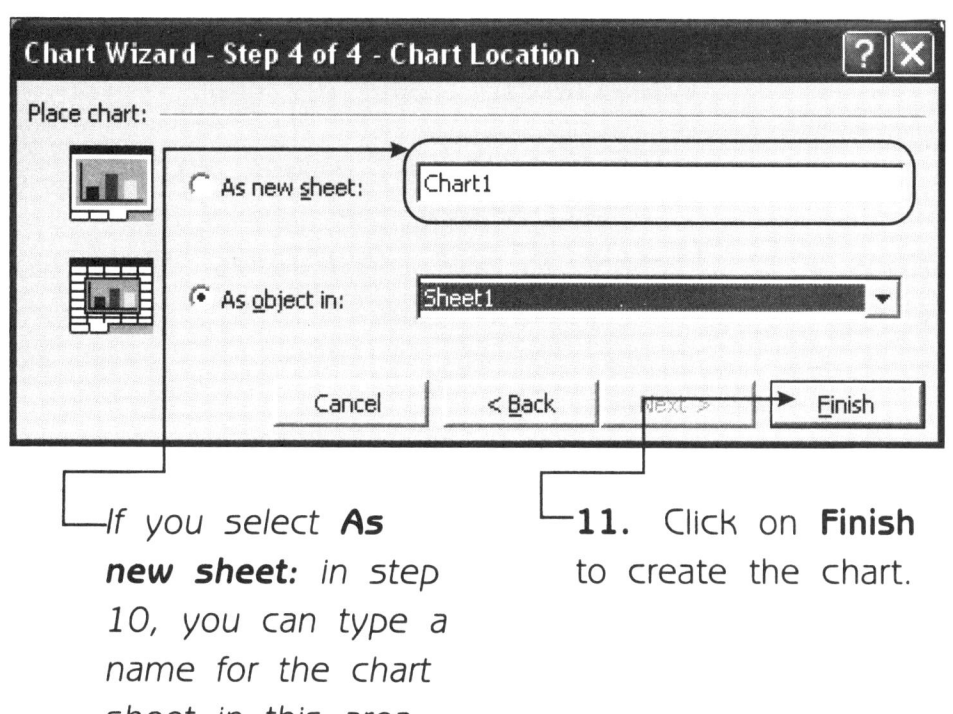

*If you select **As new sheet:** in step 10, you can type a name for the chart sheet in this area.*

11. Click on **Finish** to create the chart.

39

Drag and Drop Series

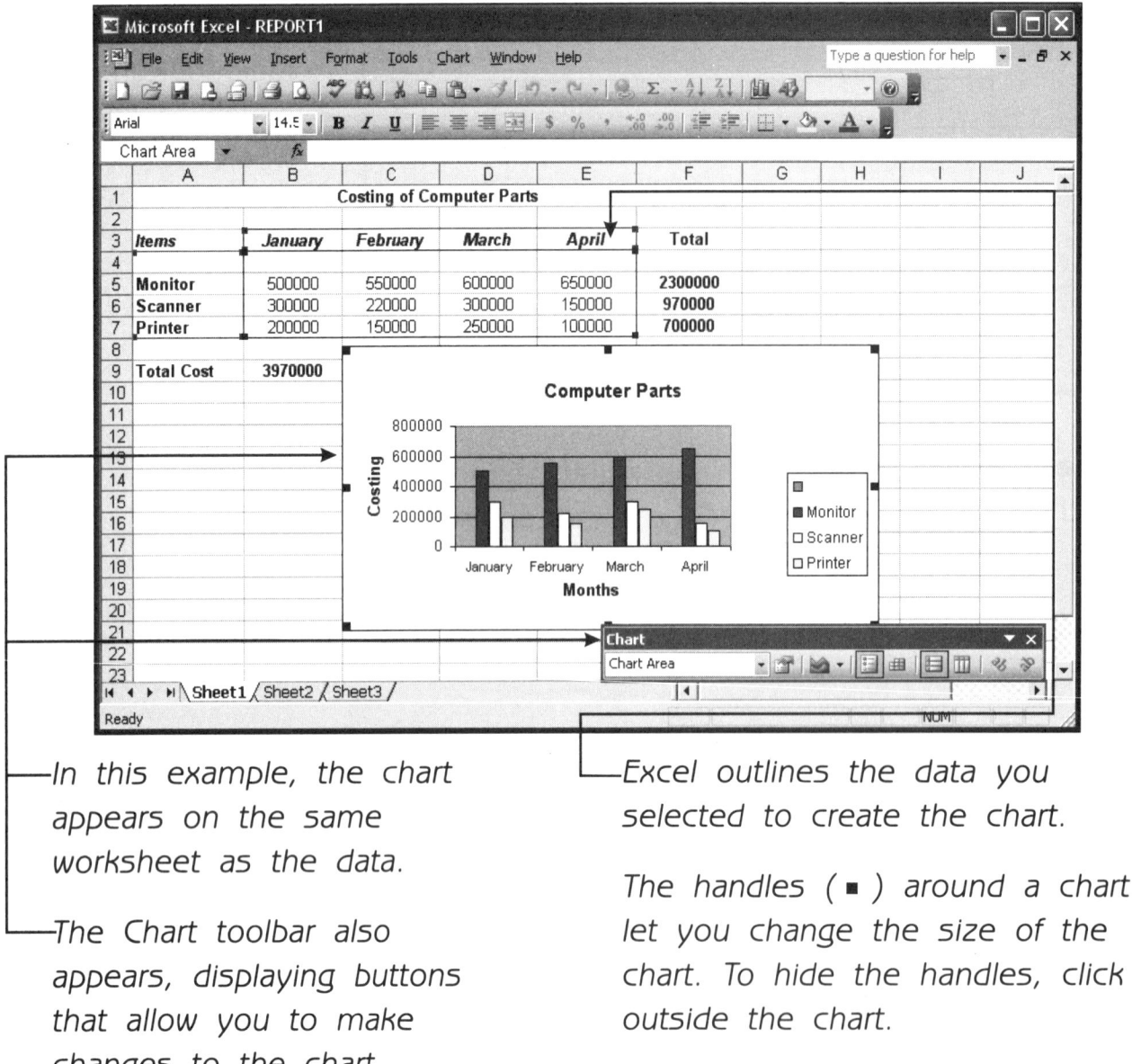

In this example, the chart appears on the same worksheet as the data.

The Chart toolbar also appears, displaying buttons that allow you to make changes to the chart.

Excel outlines the data you selected to create the chart.

The handles (■) around a chart let you change the size of the chart. To hide the handles, click outside the chart.

To Delete a Chart

1. Click on a blank area in the chart you want to delete. Handles (■) appear around the chart.

2. Press the **Delete** key on the keyboard to delete the chart.

40